# HOW TO MANAGE PROBLEM EMPLOYEES

## A Step-by-Step Guide for Turning Difficult Employees into High Performers

GLENN SHEPARD

WILEY

John Wiley & Sons, Inc.

Published by John Wiley & Sons, Inc., Hoboken, New Jersey
Published simultaneously in Canada

For general information on our other products and services or for technical support, please contact our Customer Care Department within the United States at (800) 762-2974, outside the United States at (317) 572-3993 or fax (317) 572-4002.

Wiley also publishes its books in a variety of electronic formats. Some content that appears in print may not be available in electronic books. For more information about Wiley products, visit our web site at www.wiley.com.

*Library of Congress Cataloging-in-Publication Data:*

Shepard, Glenn, 1963–
  How to manage problem employess : a step-by-step guide for turning difficult employees into high performers / Glenn Shepard.
    p.  cm.
  ISBN-13 978-0-471-73043-9 (pbk.)
  ISBN-10 0-471-73043-2 (pbk.)
  1. Problem employees.  2. Personnel management.  3. Problem employees.  4. Personnel management.  I. Title.

  HF5549.5.E42S53    2005
  658.3′045—dc22

                                 2005004377

Printed in the United States of America.
10  9  8  7  6  5  4  3  2  1

# Preface

Throughout our country's history, pastors and politicians have proclaimed they were living in precarious times. Each generation believed it lived in a critical period of American history. As we look back with the clarity of hindsight, it becomes obvious that some generations witnessed history in the making, while others lived through relatively benign times. Many events that seemed monumental have faded into the annals of history as nothing more than slight blips on the radar screen, while others changed our country forever.

The sinking of the Titanic was the greatest news story of its time, but has little historical significance today. America's failed attempt to change over to the decimal system in the 1970s had little lasting significance, even though I remember one pastor who predicted it was the end of the world. Then came the biggest much ado about nothing the world has ever seen with Y2K. I laugh when I think about how many people stockpiled food and water in preparation for social anarchy on January 1, 2000. Today I look at all the people talking on cell phones and wonder what happened to the reports that cell phones cause brain cancer. Either those reports were wrong or the world will need many more oncologists in the future.

Other events that have occurred in our lifetime have left indelible marks on us all. No one will ever forget the terrorist attacks of September 11, 2001. While many Americans don't know the name Richard Reid, we remove our shoes thanks to him as we go through security screening at an airport. Many of the significant events of our lifetime that have gone nearly unnoticed have resulted in major societal changes. As kids, my generation got into trouble for using certain words. Today, cartoon characters use words that would make a crow blush. In 2003, the U.S. Department of Labor reported 631

workplace homicides (National Census of Fatal Occupational Injuries, 2003). Metal detectors have now become a necessity in
schools and government buildings. We have to protect ourselves
against identity theft and computer viruses. We have to monitor our
children's use of the Internet to keep them safe from child molesters.

Society has changed quietly in the past few decades. Make no
mistake, however, the change has been drastic. It is not possible for
society to change the way it dresses, acts, talks, and lives without
changing the way it works. These changes have had a drastic impact
on the workplace and have necessitated a change in the way we
manage employees. Too many managers make the mistake of attempting to manage the same way they did 20 years ago. It comes as
no surprise that their management style is no longer working. The
American work ethic has declined, people don't respect authority
figures, they expect success to be handed to them on a silver platter,
they don't stay at jobs long enough to get good at them, and it's hard
to find good people to hire. Times have changed, and so must your
management style.

Managers are fighting a battle today: We are fighting a battle to
save America's work ethic, which is slowly slipping away. If we don't
get control of this downward spiral, we face the clear and present
danger of losing our greatness. We have a problem and someone
needs to fix it. I'm not arrogant enough to think I can save my country single-handedly, but I do believe one voice can make a difference. I live in Nashville, Tennessee, near the home of Andrew
Jackson. I visit his estate, the Hermitage, whenever I need inspiration. I stand by his grave and imagine what it would have been like
to hear him speak the three legendary statements that send shivers
down my spine every time I hear them:

One man with courage makes a majority.

The brave man inattentive to his duty is worth little more to his
country than the coward who deserts in the hour of danger.

Every good citizen makes his country's honor his own and cher-
ishes it not only as precious but as sacred. He is willing to risk

his life in its defense and is conscious that he gains protection while he gives it.

All managers get discouraged and ask why they put themselves through the abuse. If you're trying to answer this question, I have an answer for you. Our country needs strong leaders, and this includes strong managers. Help fight the war to keep our country strong and prosperous—one tiny battle at a time. Don't let us slip into mediocrity. Your grandchildren and their grandchildren need you to leave this country a stronger place than you found it.

In the following pages, I show you how to manage today's problem employee, run a tight ship people want to be a part of, be the best manager you can be, and reduce your stress level at the same time. If you want real solutions for the real problems in today's workplace, this is your book. This is not about empowering employees; this is about empowering managers. We'll reward good behavior and punish bad behavior. In this tough-love approach to management, we'll break some old rules and write some new ones. If you're ready to do something about your problem employees, let's get busy. Remember, you can make a difference. Our future depends on it. America needs you!

## Acknowledgments

I always swore that if I ever won an Oscar Award, I wouldn't stand on stage and bore the world while thanking everyone and their brother. Now I understand why award winners do this. We all owe a debt of gratitude we can never fully repay to people who have helped us along the way. I am seizing this opportunity to thank some of the people who have helped me. Some made modest contributions while others had immeasurable impact on this book and my life. Some have been there stretching out their hands every step of the way. Others I've never even met, but their life's work has impacted mine so directly that I felt like they were guiding me through my career. Still others helped get my career started, even though I haven't seen them in decades. Thanks to all for helping me get to where I am today.

Thanks to Bill Bryson of Kmart, who convinced me to give my first blue-light special and overcome my fear of public speaking. I don't know why he had so much confidence in a gawky 16-year-old who trembled when he held the microphone, but that one day kindled my love affair with a microphone, which has lasted 25 years and launched a career I never dreamed of having.

Thanks to Bill Mallory of Cintas, my first boss after college, who took me under his wing and taught me grassroots management; to Billy Graham for being the positive role model I and so many others long for; to Bob Scarlatta, who brokered the purchase of my first business and gave the best financial advice for a small business owner, "Don't spend a single penny you don't have to spend during your first year in business." To Carrie Herr at the University of Toledo for giving me my big break at the ripe old age of 27; to my dedicated staff, who remain nameless at their own request—you are the best employees a manager could ever hope to have; to Dave Ramsey for his daily affirmation that there's a great place to go when people are broke, and it's called "Work"; to Dennis McKenzie for his patience in managing a young problem employee named Glenn Shepard so many years ago; to Debbie O'Brien at SUNY for convincing me to create the Excellence in Management Award; to Don Smith, my scoutmaster, who pulled me aside 30 years ago and said, "I think you have leadership potential."

Thanks to Drs. Henry Cloud and John Townsend for their incredible work in *Boundaries* and all their accompanying books that have been so instrumental in my own work; to Dr. Jerry Sutton for his inspiration; to Dr. Ralph Hillman, my speech coach; to Dr. Richard Corbin of Georgia Tech, who taught me to expand my horizons and think outside the box; to Dr. Richard Quisling, voice doctor of the country music stars, for keeping my vocal chords in tune; to Hoke Reed, federal agent and friend of 25 years, for his suggestions and help on federal law; to Gloria Green of the William Morris Agency for her time, advice, and contributions; to Greg Tipps for finding PractiCount; to Hannah Gregory for her contributions and strong faith; to Ian Pierpont of Synovate for allowing me to use his data on overindulgent parents; to Joe Calloway for his advice and input; to John Eldridge for reminding men it's okay to be men in *Wild at Heart*; to John Maxwell for all his lessons in leadership; to Jud Phillips for his contributions and friendship; to Kaye LeFebvre of Scaled Composites for information on the engineering team behind the miracle of SpaceShipOne; to my Texas colleague Kent Hutchison for his support, friendship, and help; to Linda DuBay, my high school teacher who taught me how many doors a smile can open; to Matt Holt, my executive editor at John Wiley & Sons, Inc., for allowing me to write the way I speak. Matt had confidence in me, patience after my first misstep, and made this book happen; to Tamara Hummel at Wiley for her assistance with my literarily challenged punctuation deficiency; to Myron Griffin, whose immortal words "Big dreamers never sleep" are engraved on the back of my wristwatch; to Nicole Fullerton and the HR department at Fiserv for sharing their dress code boards; to Pat Miles at the University of South Alabama, for 10 years of support and standing up for me when I became a lightening rod of controversy; to Patti Sabin who was the first person to tell me I had the talent to be a professional speaker. That one comment changed my life, Patti!

Thanks to Paul Harvey, who gave me the best advice a young speaker could ever get, "First have something worth speaking about. The rest will fall in place." I didn't like it at the time, but he was right. To Rader Walker of the Nashville Rescue Mission for his time and information; to Rae Wagoner for her management wisdom, quick quips, validation, and encouragement; to Raymond Myers, for his legal prowess, professionalism, and reassurance; to Richard Williams for giving me the book that changed my life, *The Purpose-Driven Life*; to Rick Heiden at Wycliffe Bible Translators for saving me from embarrassment; to Rick Warren for writing *The Purpose-Driven Life*; to Robert P. Campbell, retired FBI agent and polygraph examiner, for his help with employee theft and the truth about lying; to Simone Blum for the book that confirmed my belief in capitalism and free enterprise, *Atlas Shrugged*; to Steve Underwood of the Tennessee Titans for the payroll information; to Tom Howard, my first business partner and venture capitalist, who gave the best management advice for a small business owner, "You have to run your own business"; to Tom Stanley and William Danko for revealing the truth about working hard and becoming successful in *The Millionaire Next Door*; to Tracie Aicogbi for watching out for my best interests; and to my friend and golf pro Wade Conway, for "A Letter to Garcia."

Finally, I must thank the thousands of managers who have attended my seminars and shared their incredible stories. You bring honor to the profession of management and it is an honor for me to serve you.

# Contents

# CHAPTER 1

# What Happened to the American Work Ethic?

This book is a hands-on tool for solving everyday problems with employees. I'm not a professor living in an ivory tower droning on and on about management theories that have little direct benefit for the frontline supervisor. I have owned my own business since 1988, and I practice what I preach. Before we can solve the problems we'll solve together in this book, we need to look at how we got to where we are. Understanding what happened and when it happened will aid in seeing that there are solutions.

I meet thousands of managers in my seminars every year. Each has a set of circumstances he or she thinks is unique. Out of the thousands of questions I'm asked, the one I hear most often is, "What ever happened to the American work ethic?" From Boston, Massachusetts, to Baton Rouge, Louisiana, it frustrates managers to no end. Debbie in New York summed it up best when she asked, "What happened while we weren't looking?" Things changed and the American work ethic took a nosedive. The problem slipped up on us and most of us didn't see it coming until it was too late. The gradual shifting of cultural, social, and economic climates in the 1990s left a legacy of a declining work ethic such as we've never seen. Let's look at what happened.

## A Country of Couch Potatoes

It's obvious that today's generations are lazier than those of the past. Perhaps this is because so many modern conveniences allow us to be lazy. For example, America has become a drive-through nation. Without ever leaving the comfort of your car, you can:

- Apply for a loan.
- Buy beer and cigarettes, groceries, or lottery tickets.
- Do your banking.
- Donate to charity.
- Drop off and pick up your dry cleaning.
- Eat.
- Get flu shots.
- Get married.
- Get photographs developed.
- Have your car washed.
- Have your oil changed.
- Have your prescriptions filled.
- Mail a letter.
- Pawn your extra stuff.
- Pay your respects to the recently departed at the drive-through viewing window of a funeral home.
- Place a bet in a casino.
- View art at a drive-through art gallery.
- Watch a movie at a drive-in theatre.

For those who find getting in the car and leaving the house too much work, we have the Internet. Without leaving the comfort of your home you can:

- Apply for a job, a car loan, a credit card, or a home mortgage
- Adopt a child (at least partially).
- Balance your checking account.
- Book an airline ticket, a cruise, or a hotel room.
- Buy CDs or DVDs, a cellular telephone, groceries, guns, movie tickets, or tickets to concerts or ballgames.
- Buy or sell stocks or shares in mutual funds.
- Buy other people's extra stuff.
- Chat online with friends, business associates, and family members (who are in the next room).
- Commit crimes.
- Consult with a doctor, a financial advisor, a lawyer, a pastor, or a psychiatrist.
- Custom configure a computer, have it built and delivered the same week.
- Do all your Christmas shopping and have presents delivered to your doorstep prewrapped.
- Do research for business or homework.
- Donate to charity.
- Hire a groomer to come to your house and groom your dog.
- Hire a dog sitter to feed and walk your dog.
- Hire a trainer to train your dog.
- Hire someone to clean your house.
- Arrange for a massage or yoga lesson.
- Hire someone to wash your car or change the oil.
- Hire someone to mow your lawn or spray for weeds.
- Hire someone to clean your chimney or air conditioning ducts.
- Get a college degree.
- Get divorced.
- Get photographs developed or prescriptions filled.

- Open a checking account or an IRA.
- Order clothes and exchange those that don't fit.
- Order flowers, pizza, wine, or groceries and have them delivered.
- Pay for and print postage labels for a package the mail carrier will pick up at your door.
- Pay your bills or taxes.
- Place a bet in a casino.
- Read a book or newspaper.
- Rent a DVD and have it delivered.
- Sell your old car or other stuff.
- Shop for and buy a new car or a house.
- Start a business.
- View art galleries.
- Watch movies.
- Take a virtual tour through a museum.
- Watch your kids in day care.

You can't buy lotto tickets online yet, but the Virginia Lottery allows state residents to purchase them by mail. If getting up off the sofa and walking to the computer requires too much effort, there's wireless Internet access (WiFi). You can surf the Web on your laptop computer using WiFi and never leave the sofa. I feel like such a dinosaur now explaining to kids how we didn't have remote controls for television sets in the old days. I knew not to go near the television when Dad was watching because I'd have to stand there and change channels. We thought the remote control was the greatest invention since air conditioning. Then doctors became concerned that remote controls made it too easy for people to watch television and never leave the sofa. Little could they have predicted where the Internet would take us. Now people can buy a new television set without leaving the sofa.

A seminar attendee in Kansas City, Missouri, had a conversation that revealed how lazy technology has allowed us to become. Her 12-year-old son didn't want to make the trip to Sedona, Arizona, to visit his grandmother. He argued, "Why do we have to go visit? We have free long distance and can talk to her any time we want." He had a good point. Just a few years ago, long distance service cost 35 cents a minute. Talking to Grandma out of state was a big deal. Now we can talk free on nights and weekends to friends or loved ones anywhere in the country. When the woman explained she wanted to see Grandma instead of just talk to her, he suggested buying a web-cam for his computer and one for Grandma. In the 1995 movie *Copycat*, Sigourney Weaver portrayed a forensic psychologist who became agoraphobic and never left her home. It seemed freakish and bizarre at the time; now it almost seems normal.

Why would anyone ever need to leave home today? The answer is to go to work. With all these modern conveniences, work is inconvenient. It's no wonder that so many Americans find it an imposition to drag out of bed and commute to work every day. If the tough get going when the going gets tough, what happens when the going gets too easy? As managers know, people can grow fat and lazy. Living in the land of milk and honey doesn't require much effort. It does, however, require self-discipline, or the milk and honey will start to show around our waistlines. We don't need to look far to see this is exactly what's happening in the United States today—both figuratively and literally.

## Too Many Castles, Too Few Kings

In 1985, I was a senior studying industrial management at Georgia Tech in Atlanta. An economics professor said, "I don't know how your generation will ever afford to buy a home with interest rates so high." I graduated and bought my first home in Nashville, Tennessee, the next year. I paid $37,000 for a two-bedroom condominium and financed it at 11 percent. The monthly payment was the same as rent on my old apartment, and I couldn't understand his gripe. The mortgage rates fell below 5 percent 20 years later. I now live in a four-bedroom house I bought later that same year. It's modest, but meets my needs just fine. Yet, I sometimes find myself doing the math to see how much more I could have purchased if the interest rate was 5 percent back then. I'm grateful the interest rates were so high. Had they been as low as they are today, I might have been tempted to take on more debt than I should have. The Federal Housing Finance Board reported that the national average one-family-house purchase price in November 2004 was over $264,000.[1] Today's 40-year-low interest rates have allowed people to buy houses their parents would never have dreamed of buying. Some of these homes are very luxurious; they're like castles with granite countertops, marble floors, bidets, jacuzzi bathtubs, crown molding, and vaulted ceilings. Add two $40,000 SUVs in a heated and air-conditioned garage and today's average Joe is living like yesterday's Joe Millionaire.

So what's the problem with living in a castle? Kings and queens live in castles. When the average Joe lives in a castle, it's easy for him to develop a false sense of accomplishment. Why would anyone want to drag out of bed and leave a warm castle for a cold factory? Every woman wants to be a queen, and every man wants to be a king. We are neither when we go to work; we are servants for hire. Contrast this to the guy who lives in a roach-infested apartment that is cold and dank in the winter. There's no air-conditioning and it's sweltering in the summer. He looks forward to going to work because it's nicer than where he lives. As our standard of living has improved and housing has become so elaborate, work just doesn't fit into the picture.

## Litigation Nation

Some blame Stella Liebeck for the litigation frenzy in this country. Stella was the 79-year-old woman a New Mexico jury awarded $2.9 million after spilling hot McDonald's coffee in her lap in 1992. She became an icon for an out-of-control tort system, but she was not the cause. The problem began 15 years earlier.

American lawyers couldn't advertise for over 200 years. That changed with a five to four U.S. Supreme Court decision in 1977.[2] Justice Lewis Powell wrote in his dissenting opinion, "Some lawyers may gain; others will suffer by the deceit of less scrupulous lawyers. Some members of the public may benefit . . . but the risk is that many others will be victimized." Justice Powell predicted the future with spine-tingling accuracy. It's too bad the other five justices didn't listen. I wonder if he ever looked back and said, "I told you this was going to happen." Lawyers spent over $311 million on television commercials in 2002. This was a 75 percent increase from 1999. If you look in any Yellow Pages you'll see a law firm that paid as much as $60,000 to buy a full-page ad. Now the big trend is advertising on the Internet. Type "class-action lawsuit" into your search engine and you'll find thousands of law firms soliciting plaintiffs.

The problem is bad enough with ambulance chasers who might lack morals but at least stay within the law. Then there's the problem with those who break the law in order to practice law by paying runners to solicit accident victims. At least they're only chasing plaintiffs who were involved in legitimate accidents. Even worse are the lawyers who create the accidents. One scam is called *swoop and squat,* in which a driver with a car full of plaintiffs-to-be pulls in front of the unknowing victim and, slams on the brakes, forcing a rear-end collision. The lawyer then sues the insurance company for whiplash on behalf of the victims.

So how does this affect you? America's out-of-control tort system raises two worrisome issues for employers. The first issue is how it affects the work ethic. The basic premise of tort law is avoiding personal accountability by assigning blame to others. We've gone from "McDonald's coffee burned me" to "McDonald's made me fat and I was an innocent victim." The second issue is that employers are the newest targets for litigation. The victim mentality is now "I lost my job through no fault of my own. I couldn't help it that I couldn't get to work on time." Listen for the following advertisement:

> Have you been wrongfully terminated? Call my office today and let us get you the money you're entitled to. Justice is your right, and we demand it because you deserve it!

Your company has a bull's-eye painted on it. The bigger your company, the more likely a lawyer will have you in his crosshairs.

## Today's Generation

Many members of today's generation are undisciplined, have no desire to grow up and accept responsibility, and have been spoiled by overindulgent parents. Each of these affects employees' behavior and consequently your actions as a supervisor.

## Back When Kids Wanted to Be like Grown-Ups

When I was a kid, we couldn't wait to grow up. Little boys had toy razors and used their dad's shaving cream to pretend to shave. I was reprimanded on numerous occasions for using my father's or grandfather's pen in my coloring books. Fancy pens were for grown-ups, and that's what I wanted to be. The first time I heard my father being excited to go Christmas shopping was on my twenty-fourth Christmas. Mom asked what they could give me and I suggested a Mont Blanc pen. Dad was overwhelmed with pride. It was the pride a dentist feels when his son graduates dental school and joins his father to practice dentistry. It was the pride an attorney feels when his son graduates law school and joins his father to practice law. I became a real man in my dad's eyes the day I asked for that pen. It indicated to Dad that I had matured sufficiently to appreciate the finer things in life. Little girls in my generation couldn't wait to grow up either. They would get into trouble for wearing their mother's makeup, lipstick, and eventually shoes and clothes. When a little girl was big enough to get her ears pierced like her mom's, she had arrived.

We were all anxious to graduate high school and leave for college. Then we were anxious to graduate college and start our lives. I took classes the summer between my junior and senior years in college so I could graduate the following spring. I was chomping at the bit to move into the real world. When I received my first American Express card my senior year, I felt validated. I returned the credit card Dad had allowed me to carry in case of an emergency, and proudly announced I no longer needed it. Members of my generation who didn't attend college also valued independence. The top priority for most was moving out and getting their own apartment. For others, it was getting married and starting a family. No matter which path we chose, we couldn't wait to take on the world. We valued independence and self-reliance.

## Now Grown-Ups Want to Be Kids

Today, there is an ever-growing population of twenty-somethings who readily admit they're in no hurry to leave home. They value leisure over independence, and are putting off growing up as long as possible. They have been labeled "youthhood," "adult-lescents," "thresholders," and part of the "Peter Pan Syndrome." The U.S. Census Bureau reported over five million unmarried couples cohabitating in 2000.[3] This used to be a thorn in parents' side. In an ironic twist of fate, many parents of twenty-somethings today wish their kids would move in with their boyfriends or girlfriends. They just want them out of the house.

Those who leave for college aren't graduating. Lingering has become such a problem that universities are almost to the point of forcing students out. Four-year degrees often take six to eight years. The University of Texas spent $22 million on a program to entice students to graduate in four years. Western Illinois University guarantees freshman their tuition won't increase as long as they finish in four years. UCLA students face expulsion for not earning a quota of credits each semester. Instead of living in crowded dorms, students today are living in luxury apartments. They're running up credit card bills for beer and pizza. They're spending Spring Break in Mexico and Christmas in Europe. In 2002, 19 percent of the people who filed for bankruptcy were college students. As social chairman of my fraternity for two consecutive years, I readily admit that we hauled more than a few kegs. We lived on beer, pizza, and chili dogs for four years. We also lived on campus in military-style dorms, walked to class, and graduated in four years. College was a stepping-stone to adulthood, not a permanent way of life.

### Boomerang Kids

Adult-lescents are now moving back in with mom and dad after graduating college. These "boomerang kids" argue that they're doing it to save money. This sounds good, but it isn't the case for most. A report from research organization Demos revealed average credit card debt for young adults ages 25 to 34 increased by 55 percent from 1992 to 2001, and 104 percent for ages 18 to 24.[4] Young adults don't learn personal responsibility and self-discipline until they're self-supportive. Having greater disposable income allows them to feed impulsive spending habits and become even more irresponsible. While the statistics don't indicate how many of these young adults live with their parents, we know it is a huge trend. David Morrison, founder and CEO of market research firm Twentysomething Inc., says that 65 percent of this year's college graduates plan to move back in with their parents after graduation.[5] Recent findings published by the American Sociological Association revealed the percentage of men who had finished school, left home, married, become financially independent, and had a child by age 30 was 65 percent in 1960. It was only 31 percent in 2000. The percentage for women fell from 77 percent to 46 percent for the same period.[6]

Another argument some boomerang kids make is that they're taking time to decide what to do with their lives. They don't want to "rush into a career they might not like." I don't buy this either. Student loan provider Nellie Mae reported that the average undergraduate student loan debt was $18,900 in 2002, a 66 percent increase from 1997.[7] Young adults with this much debt don't have the luxury of waiting to decide what they want to do with their lives. I would love to gather a room full of these overgrown adolescents and scream, "You just spent nearly $19,000 deciding what you want to do with your life. It's too late to pontificate the matter. Now get off your lazy behinds and get a real job!" As soon as the room cleared, I would love to meet with their parents and scream, "Quit enabling your kids to be so irresponsible. Cut the apron strings already!"

I heard a recent college graduate call in to a nationally syndicated financial talk show. He is living at home with his parents and having a hard time paying his student loans. When asked what he was doing with the money from his job, he explained that he had just purchased a big screen television. These young adults are developing deeply ingrained habits of irresponsibility and lack of self-control. These habits are going to be harder to break the longer they wait.

So how does this affect employers? At some point, you'll be employing these young adults. You'll have to teach them basic values such as personal responsibility. You'll also need to look more closely at twenty-something job applicants to determine what life stage they are in. Is this a young adult or an overgrown adolescent still living in the same bedroom he or she lived in at 16? Fast-food restaurants see annual employee turnover rates as high as 200 percent. A substantial part of this turnover is because teenagers fill a high percentage of these positions. They can walk out on impulse if they don't like being reprimanded. When a person has no financial obligations, employment is not a necessity. When you employ a 28-year-old still living with his parents, you are essentially employing a 28-year-old teenager; employment is not a necessity for him. All other things being equal, I'll hire a 22-year-old who is self-supportive over a 28-year-old who is mooching off mom and dad.

## Overindulgent Parents

Parents may be creating a time bomb with the potential to do more damage to the American work ethic than anything we've ever faced. Overindulgent parents are raising materialistic kids who think the world revolves around them. One current trend is called best-friend parenting. According to market research firm Synovate, 43 percent of parents surveyed want to be their kids' best friend.[8] The problem is that they're failing to be parents while trying to be best friends. One mom said she wouldn't make her child do homework or chores because it made him unhappy. Synovate also found that 40 percent of the parents would buy their kids everything they wanted if finances allowed. In the name of "I want my kids to have what I never had," parents are inflicting serious damage on their kids. Even adults who have selflessly eschewed their own materialism in the name of being a good parent have failed to see how materialistic they have made their own kids.

My father used to say, "I don't have to spank Glenn often. But when I do, I only have to do it once." When he pulled out his belt, I always got the "This is going to hurt me more than it's going to hurt you" speech. I often wanted to say, "Well, alright then. Let's trade places and we'll both be happier," but thought better of it since he was holding the belt. I resented it at the time, but appreciate it today. Dad set clear boundaries. When I violated them, I was punished. As a result, I learned to respect the boundaries. He fulfilled his duty as a parent. Too many parents today are guilty of dereliction of duty.

Parenting has gone from one extreme to the other. There was a great to-do about overcontrolling parents in the 1990s. Many of us know adults who grew up with overcontrolling parents and see the results. These individuals still relinquish control to parents who tell them when to come for Christmas, where to live, who to date, who to marry, where to work, and even what to wear. While this isn't healthy, it's not a disaster for the manager who employs them. These individuals recognize authority figures and respect boundaries. Children of overindulgent parents don't recognize authority figures or respect boundaries.

So why is it so important to teach kids boundaries? Let's look at a common misperception of adults regarding money. Most people think winning the lottery would be their key to financial independence, but it's actually the door to financial ruin. Lottery winners have a higher rate of bankruptcy and divorce than the general population. Winning the lottery doesn't make limits disappear; it just makes them harder to see until it's too late. Having a $10 million windfall seems like unlimited wealth to someone who makes $20,000 a year. However, it's not unlimited. The limit is $10 million. When someone is used to bringing home less than $400 a week, the limit is clear because it's so close. When it's so far away, we forget, deny, or procrastinate in dealing with the fact that we will inevitably have to pay the piper someday. The same is true with the child of overindulgent parents. When a child never hears *no*, it's natural for him to believe there's no limit. Mom and dad are a blank checkbook. No matter how many times parents tell a child they can't afford the new Sony Play Station, the child believes they can. When parents don't set limits or define boundaries, children don't learn to delay gratification or impulse control. These kids are now entering the workforce. Their parents are already in the workforce. Can you imagine trying to set boundaries with adults who don't think it's necessary to set boundaries with their own children?

## A Pill-Popping Nation

In his best-selling book, *Shut Up, Stop Whining, and Get a Life*, Larry Winget writes, "People are becoming more and more tolerant of whiners. It is so commonplace we hardly notice it any more."[9] He's right. We became a *Jerry Springer* nation in the 1990s when trash television talk shows became all the rage. People love to whine and some of them apparently enjoy listening to others whine. Somewhere along the way, we took it further. The United States has become a nation of hypochondriacs. Every day there seems to be a new sickness. Turn on your television and you'll find a treatment for whatever ails you. Commercials tout pills for allergies, arthritis, attention deficit disorder, attention deficit hyperactivity disorder, cancer, depression, diarrhea, dry eyes, gas, hair loss, heartburn, high blood pressure, high cholesterol, insomnia, lack of sexual desire, sexually transmitted diseases, seasonal affective disorder, and toenail fungus. If you don't think anything is wrong with you, keep watching and you will change your mind. I find myself actually craving a little purple pill and I don't even know what it does. When the dot-com boom of the 1990s created so many overnight millionaires, I sometimes felt inadequate because I wasn't a young millionaire. Now I feel inadequate because I'm missing out on pill popping. Maybe there's something wrong with me for not thinking there's something wrong with me. I actually have pill envy. Who could possibly feel like working when we're so sick? And who could find the time when we're so busy popping pills?

## Blue Handicapped Parking Placards

If pills aren't your thing, look at what's hanging from the rearview mirror of the car next to you. The blue handicapped parking placards are out of control. There was a time when motorists wanted to have the best car on the road. Now they want the best parking spot. The California Department of Motor Vehicles has issued 400,000 of these blue placards in Los Angeles County alone and estimate there may be an additional 800,000 fakes. The problem is so bad that they formed a Disabled Placard Taskforce. I have no problem with handicapped parking placards for people with disabilities; I have a problem with abuse of these placards. Where does it end? I recently saw one hanging off the mirror of a Corvette. I own a 1994 Corvette and it's an ordeal for me to get my 6'4" frame out of it. I believe anyone who can pull this off can walk across a parking lot. The problem with giving special attention to any group is not just political, ideological, and economic—it's also mathematical. Eventually, so many people will find a way to join the group that it will no longer be special. The proliferation of blue placards has now created infighting within the protected class. A seminar attendee in Texas told me her company was forced to designate more handicapped parking spaces as more employees obtained the blue placards. Now an employee has a doctor's note explaining she needs the handicapped parking spot closest to the building. Her disability is apparently worse than the other employees' disabilities. Is this disability envy? Again I ask, "Where does it end?"

## Scooter Envy

This conundrum is not solely the result of medical or legal issues. It's also good business for companies that pander to those who have, or believe they have, a disability. Watch the commercials for scooters for people who are "mobility impaired." These scooters look like golf carts with an attitude. Now I have scooter envy. If you can't afford your own $2,000 scooter, go to your nearest Super Wal-Mart and use one of theirs. I now look both ways before crossing the main aisle at Wal-Mart because I'm afraid a scooter will run me down. Wal-Mart knows what they're doing. Their scooters have big shopping baskets that the rider can fill with products as he or she cruises the store. I've watched these people leave the store many times. Most get up and walk out on the strength of their own two legs.

The people who are too unhealthy to work aren't working for you. We can safely assume many of them live on disability or some other form of government assistance. Your employees are still affected by this. When those who pull their own weight resent those who can but don't, morale will suffer. How many times have you heard a hardworking employee complain, "I'm sick and tired of busting my behind so my tax dollars can support someone who doesn't want to work"? When we see people abusing the system, we wonder if the joke's on us for working so hard. Eventually we start to wonder if the best approach might be "If you can't beat 'em, join 'em."

## Grunge Music and Gangster Rap

Go back to the 1980s. Serpentine necklaces, BMWs, and gold nugget rings symbolized a decade of conspicuous consumption. One of the hottest selling business books was *Dress for Success*.[10] America was a hard working country that valued success. The silver screen portrayed our admiration for those who worked hard and succeeded in *Working Girl, Top Gun, An Officer and a Gentleman,* and *Flashdance*. Pop music was as much about looking good as sounding good. ZZ Top sang about women going crazy over sharp dressed men. Bands such as Bon Jovi, Def Leppard, and Motley Crue teased their hair, donned spandex, and wore more makeup than the women they chased.

Fast forward to Seattle in the 1990s. In a backlash to the glam rock of the 1980s, Generation X embraced a new sound called grunge rock. Instead of dressing up, they dressed down. They traded their thin leather ties and parachute pants for flannel shirts and boots. The new music from groups such as Nirvana and Pearl Jam was angry. The first female rocker to jump into the angst was Alanis Morissette. She wore no makeup and her hair always looked greasy. In her hit song "Ironic," she whined about how awful life was. The lyrics described a fly in her glass of wine, a man who died the day after winning the lottery, another man whose plane crashed on his first flight, traffic jams, rain on her wedding day, and meeting the man of her dreams only to discover he was married.

The first time I heard this song on the radio, the deejay remarked, "How depressing is that? Doesn't it just make you want to go out and kill yourself?" I thought, "I miss ABBA!" While grunge rock was riling up the rockers, rap and hip-hop were also turning dark. Happy songs such as "U Can't Touch This" were replaced with gangster rap. Lyrics made light of killing police officers and glorified drugs and violence. Music went from an era when people dressed up and chose to be happy to an era when they dressed down and felt sorry for themselves.

Young people were consumed with feelings of despair and disillusionment but had little reason to feel that way. Most actually had it quite good. Marketers laughed their way to the bank as millions of young people spent a fortune on clothes that made them look like they had no money to spend. The generation that came of age during this dark time is now in their twenties and thirties and has entered the workforce by the millions. Some of your employees today have had that "poor pitiful me" mentality engrained in their psyche since childhood. They still have a chip on their shoulders but don't know why.

## Television Began Ridiculing Authority Figures

Authority figures were portrayed in a positive manner for about the first 40 years of television. In the 1950s, *Leave It to Beaver* painted Ward Cleaver as a father in charge. Robert Young was reverently portrayed in the title of his series, *Father Knows Best*. In the 1960s, little Opey never faced a dilemma Andy Griffith couldn't magically make go away. Even the most bizarre family on the block respected Dad on *The Addams Family*. Mike Brady came to the rescue any time the *Brady Bunch* faced the slightest threat in the 1970s. Even Fonzie was respectful toward Mr. and Mrs. Cunningham on *Happy Days*. Hollywood began to experiment with family units in the 1980s, but remained respectful. Bill Cosby guided one of the first Black prime time television families through all life's ups and downs. Single dad Phillip Drummond was the go-to guy for Gary Coleman in *Different Strokes*. Will Smith knew not to push Uncle Phil too far in *The Fresh Prince of Bel Aire*. Television also treated career success positively in the 1980s. Bill Cosby played a doctor as Heathcliff Huxtable, while his wife Claire was an attorney. Will Smith's Uncle Phil was an attorney. *L.A. Law* portrayed attorneys so positively that law schools across the United States saw enrollment shoot up. Phillip Drummond was an executive.

Just like popular music, television took an abrupt turn in the 1990s. Suddenly authority figures were the brunt of the jokes. In 1993, Kelsey Grammer began an 11-year run as Frasier where he and his brother Niles were successful psychiatrists. Yet, the two doctors were the idiots, while housekeeper Daphne, grumpy old Dad, and even the dog Eddie were the smart ones. In 1996, Ray Romano emerged as a loyal husband, father, and successful writer in *Everybody Loves Raymond*. Yet, he was the brunt of nearly every joke from day one. In 1998, Ted Danson debuted in his newest sitcom *Becker*. Since Dr. Becker lived alone and had no family to mock him, his employees did. From its 1998 debut, *King of Queens* portrayed Kevin

James's character Doug Heffernan as a bumbling, overgrown thirty-something, and his father-in-law as completely inept.

Cartoons are even worse. *The Simpsons* mocks every authority figure. I personally find the show entertaining. You just can't dislike an affable guy like Homer Simpson. Nonetheless, it sends a clear message: Homer is an imbecile. Police Chief Clancy Wiggum is overweight, lazy, and not too bright. Mayor Quimby is a woman chaser and heavy drinker. Principal Seymour Skinner is not so stable and still lives with his domineering mother. Reverend Lovejoy is arrogant and condescending. The character portrayed in the most negative light is Homer's boss, Mr. Burns. At least *The Simpsons* is rated G. In 1997, the first R-rated cartoon debuted on the Comedy Channel. *South Park* follows four foul-mouthed delinquents who make fun of everything from drugs to child molestation. The issue is not whether television changes how people think, but whether television reflects how we already think. The popularity of shows mocking authority figures and high achievers illustrates what Americans are thinking; even if television is not the catalyst, it is an indicator.

## People Are Looking for a Free Ride

I tried watching the reality television show *The Osbournes*. I couldn't follow the dialogue because the producers had to bleep out so many of Ozzy's words. He definitely doesn't get the Father-of-the-Year award. Still, there's one thing no one can take away from Ozzy. The man is not afraid of working. He took his career seriously and now enjoys the fruits of his labor. Millions of people have a foul mouth like Ozzy's; I find it ironic the only four-letter word that offends them is W-O-R-K. Americans are obsessed with finding ways to get by without working. There is a growing number of Americans who want the government to support them. Even working Americans are looking for ways to live off the government. We all know someone who has attempted to get disability, workman's compensation, or unemployment benefits. Even retired Americans are trying to get a free ride in their golden years. Attorneys advise older clients how to give their money to their kids in order to get Medicaid to pay the nursing home bills. Television commercials for the $2,000 scooters promise to help get Medicare to pay for them. We saw the most unscrupulous Americans emerge after the September 11 terrorist attacks. They collected Social Security benefits by filing false claims on family members who never existed. People who can't finagle a way to live off the government directly will try it indirectly by playing the lottery. If people would put as much effort in to finding work as they put in to finding ways to avoid work, the unemployment rate would be next to nothing.

Another example is the latest reality television shows, which are about getting something for nothing, and getting it immediately. In one hour or less, we see people find the perfect husband or wife, have their houses remodeled, or get total physical makeovers. I find it amazing how many people will drink cows' blood, lay in a box of snakes, or jump off a building for the chance to win a one-time prize of $50,000. Yet, so many people won't get out of bed in the morning and show up for a job that pays $50,000 a year.

## The Death of Laissez-Faire

Our country was founded on the principle of laissez-faire. This doctrine opposes government interference with business and holds that capitalism works best when left alone. One of my personal heroes validated my belief in this system on June 21, 2004, when he launched the first private manned vehicle beyond the earth's atmosphere. Burt Rutan succeeded in doing with 30 engineers, only 5 of whom were full time, and $25 million, what took NASA thousands of employees and billions of dollars to do. This historic victory for free enterprise was made even sweeter by the source of the funding. The money for Mr. Rutan's SpaceShipOne did not come from a government grant; it came from another entrepreneur who also made history with a small team a few decades earlier. That entrepreneur was Paul Allen. His partner was Bill Gates, and the company was Microsoft. As an entrepreneur, management consultant, pilot, proud American, and staunch believer in free enterprise, my eyes welled with tears when I heard that Mr. Rutan's team succeeded. I knew history had been made, just as it was in 1903 when Orville Wright piloted the first powered airplane. Mr. Rutan only had to fill out two government forms in order to complete his mission. He proved free enterprise works best with minimal government interference.

Our country's solid foundation of laissez-faire first began to crack for employers in 1938. For over 160 years, politicians generally steered clear of labor laws. This changed drastically with the Fair Labor Standards Act (FLSA). The FLSA was part of President Franklin D. Roosevelt's New Deal, which also included the creation of welfare, unemployment benefits, and Social Security. Among other things, the FLSA created a minimum hourly wage and required time and a half for hourly employees working over 40 hours a week. As always happens when government interferes too much with private business, the FLSA backfired. It actually hurt many of the workers it was intended to help. Politicians could have prevented this with a little common sense and basic knowledge of how business works. For example, pretend you manage a distribution center. Your warehouse employees make $10 an hour. You need 20 people to work an extra 15 hours per week for the next six weeks. The FLSA forces you to pay them $15 an hour for overtime, for a cost of $27,000 excluding payroll taxes. Alternatively, you could bring in 20 temporary employees (temps), pay them $10 an hour, and save $9,000. Which are you going to do? Hire the temps, of course. Now imagine one of your employees is expecting his first child, and really needs the extra hours. You explain you would prefer to use him, but he's too expensive at $15 an hour. He volunteers to work the extra time at his regular rate of $10 an hour. Sorry, you can't do it. The FLSA will not allow him to work the extra hours he chooses, at the rate he chooses to work.

A single mom was furious with me after discussing this during my seminar at the University of Wisconsin in Kenosha. She bellowed, "Glenn, you don't understand how hard it is to feed three kids when you're a single mom. My company is stingy and I hardly get any overtime. I need every hour of overtime I can get!" She proved my point. If the law didn't make her so expensive, she might get more hours from her "stingy" employer. She also inadvertently brought up a point I missed. There could be a personal conflict of interest between a manager and employee when overtime is involved. Many managers are paid bonuses based on how well they control costs. The manager wants to make as much as she can for her family, too. If she has to choose between what's best for her kids and what's best for her employee's kids, she's not going to pay overtime.

Also consider the fatigue factor. If I'm forced to pay 150 percent of an employee's regular hourly rate, then I expect 150 percent productivity. I won't get it. Productivity goes down the longer an employee works. Just look at yourself. Do you get more done in the first hour of your day when you're fresh, or in the last hour when you're exhausted? Paying 150 percent of an employee's hourly pay in exchange for 75 percent productivity is not a wise investment. The more expensive something is, the less of it I can afford. This is why companies want to avoid paying overtime. The government is preventing many of the people who want to work more than 40 hours a week from being able to do so.

## The Assault on Employment-at-Will

The next crack in laissez-faire was the assault on employment-at-will. This legal doctrine means an employer can fire an employee at any time and without cause. Employees working under collective bargaining agreements or individual employment contracts are excluded. The federal and state governments have launched an all out assault on this doctrine over the past four decades.

### The Federal Government and the Assault on Employment-at-Will

The employment-at-will doctrine survived mostly intact until the civil rights movement of the 1960s. The Equal Pay Act of 1963 protected employees, effectively women, from sex-based wage discrimination. Title VII of the Civil Rights Act of 1964 prohibited employment discrimination based on race, color, religion, sex, or national origin. The Age Discrimination in Employment Act of 1967 prohibited employment discrimination based on age for anyone 40 or older. No one should be denied employment or advancement because of religion, skin color, sex, age, or national origin. These laws are moral and just; abuse of these laws is not. As we discuss later, people have abused and exploited each of these laws. Now fast forward to the 1990s. The cracks in employment-at-will turned into a hemorrhage. It began with the Americans with Disabilities Act of 1990. Next came the Civil Rights Act of 1991 that provided monetary damages up to $300,000 for intentional discrimination and made sexual harassment a household term. Next came the Family Medical Leave Act of 1993, which requires covered companies to give employees up to 12 weeks unpaid leave each year for certain personal issues. Finally, the Sarbanes Oxley Act of 2002 put corporate CEOs and their auditors in the legal hot seat. In *The Daily Drucker,* Peter Drucker correctly questioned how this legislation will affect the bond between an employee and his or her supervisor.[11] I predict that it will ultimately be used as an argument for wrongful termination. An employee terminated for good cause will falsely claim that his boss knew he was about to blow the whistle on some alleged fraudulent activity and use the Sarbanes Oxley Act in his defense. Now in addition to making false workers' compensation claims or false accusations of discrimination or harassment, problem employees can falsely claim they were fired to cover up accounting fraud that doesn't exist, and cost employers thousands in legal fees to defend themselves.

### California and the Assault on Employment-at-Will

Although the bulk of the state assaults began in the 1980s, California began theirs in a 1959 court case. The court ruled that an employee cannot be fired for refusing to commit an illegal act.[12]

This created the first commonly recognized exception to employment-at-will, called a *public policy exception.* The majority of the states now recognize this exception. The second exception is an *implied contract,* which can be argued to exist when a policy manual states that an employee will receive a verbal warning followed by a written warning, and so on. Statements made to employees such as "Your job is safe as long as you do it well" have also been used as a basis for an implied contract. The majority of the states now recognize this exception. The third exception is the *covenant of good faith exception.* It is the most controversial and far-reaching. In a case involving American Airlines, a California court ruled in favor of an employee simply because he had been with the company for 18 years.[13] The court stated, "Termination of employment . . . after such a period of time offends the implied-in-law covenant of good faith and fair dealing." The California Supreme Court later overturned this, but the damage was done. Eleven states now recognize this exception.

### Montana Fired the Shot Heard around the Country

The greatest damage to employment-at-will came in 1987 when the Montana legislature passed the Montana Wrongful Discharge from Employment Act. It requires employers to have "good cause" for termination. Even though the law specified that failure to satisfactorily perform job duties is good cause, the Montana Supreme Court trampled on this stipulation in a 2001 case. An office clerk at a plywood mill sued her employer for wrongful termination. During an audit, it was revealed that a substantial amount of cash was missing, checks did not match invoices, and deposits slips were not adding up. She was offered a position in the mill, but resigned. Her attorney argued that the employer did not have good cause for discharge because she was not properly trained, had not been properly evaluated, and the company didn't have established procedures for proper performance of the job. The district court ruled in favor of the company. She appealed, and the Montana Supreme Court ruled in her favor, essentially saying it was the employer's fault she didn't do her job.

Note that she was never fired. She resigned and still sued for wrongful termination. Montana law gives an employee this right under the doctrine of constructive discharge. It allows an employee to voluntarily quit and claim he or she was forced to because the environment was so difficult. Montana amended their wrongful discharge law in 2001 to eliminate all references to employment-at-will except for probationary employees. The amendment also created a default probationary period of six months during which an employer can fire at will. While this sounds beneficial to employers, it will only serve as ammunition for more lawsuits by employees who are terminated shortly after probation ends. Employees will be on their best behavior while on probation. As soon as they feel secure, their real personalities will emerge. A manager who attended my seminar last year told of her experience: A worker from a temp service had perfect attendance for 10 weeks and the company hired her. She then had 37 absences in a 34-week period, 25 of which were unscheduled.

Montana law also specifies punitive damages for any employer who attempts to prevent a former employee from gaining new employment by giving a bad reference. The law states that truthful statements for reason of discharge are allowed. A terminated employee, however, is not likely to agree with the reason his employer gave for firing him. The Montana Supreme Court wrote that the terminated employee might have "an independent cause of action for intentional infliction of emotional distress." Montana law even states that employers have a duty to furnish upon demand of a discharged employee a written statement explaining the reasons for termination. An employer who fails to do so is guilty of a criminal misdemeanor.

Is the hair standing up on the back of your neck? Employers have gone from over 200 years of being able to fire at will to being required (in at least one state) to have cause for employee termination approved by politicians and judges They face criminal prosecution for not explaining the cause in writing. Laissez-faire is not fairing well these days. More labor laws have been passed in your lifetime than in the first 160 years of our country's history. Politicians and judges are killing the American work ethic.

## Conclusion

This is the state of affairs today, and it's not a pretty picture. We've become a nation of lazy hypochondriacs who aren't responsible for our actions, don't want to grow up, feel sorry for ourselves, are addicted to convenience, conditioned to disrespect and mock authority figures, are obsessed with finding ways to get by without working, looking to get rich quick with the least amount of effort possible, in a legal system which has launched an all out assault on employers' rights.

Are you angry? You have a right to be. Are you feeling a little hopeless? Don't be. It's time for you and me to get down to the business of saving our country's greatness before judges and politicians drag us into mediocrity. Now that you know how we got to where we are today, let's look at how to get to where we want to be tomorrow.

# CHAPTER 2

# Becoming the Manager You Need to Be

**A** soldier has to prepare for war before he encounters the enemy. He does not have time to study military strategies and theories once the battle is raging. The same is true for managers. You're about to fight a battle in the trenches, while politicians and professors sit around talking about it. It's an uphill battle where political trends, social climates, government interference, an entitlement mentality, general apathy, poor parenting, spoiled brats, and overall laziness are your enemies. You and I must win our managerial battles. Our country's future depends on it. Before we talk about your problem employees, let's prepare you for battle.

## Is This Job Right for You?

I hear thousands of firsthand stories about how badly people behave. I met a manager in New York whose employee tried to stab her in the throat with scissors. A manager in Ohio told me her employee stuck a shotgun in his mouth and took his life after losing his job. A police officer in Arkansas responded to a bomb threat at a factory, only to discover an employee phoned it in to force an evacuation so that his boss wouldn't know he was late to work. Managing is not a job for the faint of heart. There's nothing shameful about deciding that you don't want to fight this battle. Those who do choose to fight it occasionally have doubts. All managers come to a point where they ask why they're putting themselves through the abuse. Perhaps your spouse has asked you this question. It's a question you need to answer for yourself. My answer in the preface was because America needs you, but that won't be enough reason for everyone.

A nurse in Illinois shared her struggle with me. She had been with her organization nearly 20 years and recently assumed a management position over 70 nurses. She was salaried and working 50 hours a week. Her pay came out to only 99 cents per hour more than one of the nurses she supervised, and she wasn't sure if it was worth the added workload. A woman in Pennsylvania found a more personal reason to be a manager. She had previously worked with children who had developmental disabilities, and she loved it. She reluctantly took a management position within the same organization and hated it. Her face lit up when she told me about the children she helped and she frowned when she told me about her employees. Her husband watched her cry too many nights as she struggled with the issue. He wanted her to go back to what she enjoyed, and I agreed with him. As we talked, she decided there was one good reason to put up with the hassles that came with managing others: She believed the good work her organization did was too important to risk letting it fall into the hands of bad managers. The added burden of management was worth it to her in order to help the children.

A widow in Alabama was in a different quandary. She had been a nurse her entire career and loved it. She left nursing because of health problems and proudly told me she had beaten cancer more than once. She had managed her late husband's dry cleaning business for the past five years and hated it. She didn't like confrontation, was disheartened by the poor work ethic of the younger generation, and didn't like the business. She was miserable and asked what I thought she should do. I recommended she read Dan Miller's *48 Days to the Work You Love*.[1] I stopped shy of telling her to get out of management because that's a decision only she can make. She just needed someone to tell her it was okay to make a change.

Fourteen-hour days and seven-day workweeks are not unusual for me. It is not always like that, but it does happen. People ask how I stand the hectic travel schedule and remain so upbeat in spite of hearing everyone's problems. They want to know my secret for looking so much younger than my age. I'm going to share my secret with you. It's a secret I learned from five of my role models—Paul Harvey, Peter Drucker, Billy Graham, George Burns, and Norman Vincent Peale. My secret is that I haven't worked in years. When you find the work you love, you'll never have to work another day in your life. Paul Harvey signed a 10-year contract extension with ABC Radio Networks in 2000 at the age of 82. When asked how he pulled it off, he said, "I lied. I told them I was 55!" Each of these great men achieved unfathomable heights of success because of their passion for their chosen careers. Each could have easily afforded to retire at 65, but chose to continue working into their eighties, and even nineties. George Burns was scheduled to perform in Las Vegas on his 100th birthday and came close to making it.

I love what I do. It's more than a career; it's my calling. I love knowing my country will be a better place because I have worked and lived in it. I can't imagine doing anything else (other than being a taste tester for Krispy Kreme doughnuts, replacing Keith Richards in the Rolling Stones, or test driving new Corvettes). I love meeting people, hearing their stories, and helping them solve their problems. (Notice I didn't say, "Solving their problems for them.") I feel validated with every round of applause and by each person who asks me to sign a book. I am humbled by the letters and e-mails I receive from people all over the United States who tell me how I've helped them. I didn't choose my job; it chose me.

So what about you? Do you have conviction? Do you have what it takes to be a strong manager? Are you sure this is what you want to do? Are you prepared to make our country stronger and better? If so, let's get you ready to rumble.

## Brandish Your Weapon and Hope You Never Have to Use It

You're not on the same level as your employees; you're their manager. Employees can behave badly only if you allow it. The problem some managers create for themselves is the same problem best-friend parents create: True friendship is not a superior-subordinate relationship. Parents are an authority figure first. No matter how close they are to their children, they can never truly be their child's best friend. When parents fail to assume the authority role in their children's lives, we see how difficult these children become. When managers don't assume the authority role, their employees become even more difficult.

President Theodore Roosevelt said, "A wise man walks softly and carries a big stick." Although he was referring to the United States' role in world affairs, this could have also applied to managers. People in President Roosevelt's time respected authority. They knew they would be held accountable for breaking rules. Murderers didn't get off the hook because they were abused as children. Shoplifters didn't avoid prosecution by claiming an addiction to stealing. Employers didn't keep bad employees out of fear of wrongful termination lawsuits.

Problem employees today assume they'll never be terminated; they don't believe they're expendable. If you've been in management long enough to fire a few people, recall how many were surprised. They never thought it would happen, despite multiple warnings. Today it's necessary to flex your muscles before you have to use them. The ultimate weapon managers have is the ability to terminate employment. Let your employees know you hope never to have to use this last resort, but will if it becomes necessary. It will be their choice. As a pastor in Memphis, Tennessee, put it, "I've never fired anyone, but I have helped employees make the decision they've already made for both of us."

## America Is Desperate for Strong Leaders

People today are yearning for strong leaders. They want men and women who make them feel secure. Political parties are struggling to find strong, charismatic candidates. Neither Al Gore nor John Kerry exhibited John F. Kennedy's charisma. Neither George Bush nor Bob Dole exhibited Ronald Reagan's caliber of leadership. I first noticed this unfed hunger for strong authority figures in 1999, when Minnesota elected Jesse "The Body" Ventura governor. Ventura is a former U.S. Navy SEAL, Vietnam veteran, and wrestler. He lacked extensive political experience but abounded with charisma. Even his political opponents recognized that he exuded strength and confidence.

I met a limo driver in New York City who had driven Mayor Rudy Giuliani. He seemed to be a fan and I ended our conversation with, "So Giuliani is a pretty nice guy?" He snapped, "Hell no. He's a mean son of a bitch!" I asked why he didn't like Giuliani, and he corrected me with, "Oh, I love him. He's exactly what New Yorkers needed, especially on 9/11." This driver told the story better than I ever could. Americans crave strong leaders. We saw it again in California in 2003. The state known for its political correctness and progressive social views recalled politically correct Governor Gray Davis and replaced him with Arnold "The Terminator" Schwarzenegger. Donald Trump began captivating viewers with the reality television show *The Apprentice*. Americans immediately began tuning in to hear him calmly say, "You're fired." Trump became the corporate version of Clint Eastwood's Dirty Harry as he coolly pulled the trigger each week. People were tired of ridiculous terms such as "downsizing, rightsizing, reducing payroll" or "we're freeing you up for other opportunities." They finally got to see a manager who would say it like it is.

## Why You Must Liberate Your Organization of Dysfunctional Employees

If animals are allowed to run the zoo, it will turn into a jungle. The law of the jungle is survival of the fittest: Eat or be eaten. In an unruly and out-of-control organization, the law becomes survival of the most obnoxious and dysfunctional. Healthy, responsible, productive employees can't exist within a dysfunctional environment. They might try to tough it out for a while, but this will never be a permanent solution. Eventually, they'll do one of two things:

1. Go with the "if you can't beat 'em, join 'em" philosophy.
2. Leave for greener pastures.

When a power void exists, someone always steps in to fill the void. This someone is usually a bully who picks on weaker individuals. Weakness invites aggression; strength repels it. This is why the ultimate deterrent to problem employees is strong management.

## You Must Lead by Example

Harry Truman had a sign on his desk in the White House Oval Office that read, "The buck stops here." He didn't look for someone to blame when things got ugly; he took responsibility for his actions. When you're the leader of the free world, it's difficult to shirk responsibility. No wonder the phrase "Give 'em hell, Harry" was heard so often.

A recent addition to my very short list of leaders who are, as Wayne and Garth from *Saturday Night Live* put it, "worthy," is Ron Serpas. He is the police chief in Nashville, Tennessee. He is a Cajun from New Orleans, Louisiana, who brought the chutzpah our city needed. He knows the only way to lead is by example. Unlike his predecessors who wore suits to work, he proudly wears a uniform like any patrol officer. He drives a patrol car and carries a ticket book. When he sees a traffic violation, he'll pull the offender over. When asked why the head of a police department with over 1,200 officers would do something as mundane as write traffic tickets, he responded, "Because I'm a police officer. Enforcing the law is what we do."

Recently, he faced what might have been the defining moment of his career. His 26-year-old son Dustin was arrested for DUI by the Vanderbilt University Police Department. They found him passed out in his car while it was still running. Five weeks later, Dustin was arrested again. This time the arresting officer was John Pepper of the Metropolitan Nashville Police Department. I immediately thought about the managers who tell me they're not allowed to hold a problem employee accountable because the employee's parents own the company. I wondered what Officer Pepper thought when he realized who he was arresting. Imagine how you'd feel in this situation. Would you worry about your career? If Officer Pepper knew Chief Serpas, I suspect he had no problem carrying out his duties.

Chief Serpas was in Los Angeles, California, at the International Association of Chiefs of Police conference when he received the news. Imagine how embarrassing this must have been. People in Tennessee are sensitive about the ethics of our leaders. On the positive side, we had Sheriff Buford Pusser of the *Walking Tall* movies. Tennessee was also home to President Andrew Johnson, who was impeached (but later acquitted) for high crimes and misdemeanors long before Bill Clinton was born. We saw Governor Ray Blanton arrested by the FBI and charged with extortion and conspiracy to sell pardons and paroles during the 1970s. Nashville's police department has been under increased scrutiny recently for the handling of DUI arrests of numerous local celebrities from Tennessee Titans quarterback Steve McNair to country music star Wynona Judd. We watched closely to see how Chief Serpas would respond to his son's arrest. He remained calm and told reporters "It is obvious . . . that Dustin didn't get the message after being arrested . . . last month. On a personal level, as a father, Dustin has seriously betrayed my trust and confidence with these two arrests. Nevertheless, I love my son. We will have a long, serious talk when I return to town this week."

Chief Serpas recently demonstrated his leadership-by-example style again when air tasers were introduced to the department. These nonlethal weapons incapacitate a person by shooting two small probes into the skin sending 50,000 volts to temporarily incapacitate the nervous system. This allows police officers to subdue violent suspects without the use of deadly force. Air tasers have recently come under scrutiny in other cities after some unfortunate incidents. To demonstrate the weapon's safety, Chief Serpas volunteered to be shot with one. Local television stations taped the demonstration as 50,000 volts shot through his body. How can one argue a weapon is dangerous when the chief allows himself to be shot with it? He silenced the critics with a display of strong leadership.

The problem with weak leaders is that the buck doesn't stop or start with them. Just as animals can smell fear, people can sense insincerity. When this happens, people will comply but not commit.

The only way to lead is by example. Fortunately for Nashville's police department, Chief Serpas is a strong leader. He knows he must lead by example in order to fight crime. Fortunately for his son, Ron Serpas is a strong father. He knows that holding a child accountable is the only way to change his behavior.

## Choose Your Battles Carefully

The most difficult choice you'll ever have to make is choosing your battles. You need to answer three questions:

1. Which battles can be won?
2. Which battles do I have to win?
3. Which battles are best not to fight?

You can't win all battles. Sometimes it's better to walk away a winner than to fight and lose. If a mugger sticks a gun in your back and demands your money, give it to him. This is one fight you're not likely to win as long as he has the weapon and you are unarmed. Other battles can be won, but the price of winning may be too high. For example, taking a customer to small claims court over an unpaid $20 invoice is unwise when the court cost is $75.

An example often brought up by managers is employees who smoke. Thirty years ago, smoking was acceptable. Allowing smokers to light up at their desks today will run off nonsmokers. You're not legally required to provide smokers a place to smoke. However, failing to do so would probably cause you to lose employees who smoke. A reasonable solution is to forbid smoking in the office but allow it outside. The next battle is how many smoke breaks to allow. If smokers take 10 breaks per day and nonsmokers take only 2, we have an issue of fairness. We need to hold everyone to the same number of breaks regardless of what they choose to do while on break. The next battle will be the nonsmoker who complains about the cigarette odor from the smoker. This is a battle you should allow the smoker to win. We all sit next to smokers on airplanes, in movie theaters, and even at church. Expecting you to provide a smoke-free office is reasonable. Expecting smokers not to smell like smoke is not. Let's tally the score on the four battles:

|  | Smokers | Non-Smokers |
|---|---|---|
| Smoking in the office | | ✓ |
| Smoking outside the building | ✓ | |
| Limiting breaks for smokers to the same as non-smokers | | ✓ |
| Cigarette odor | ✓ | |

Even law enforcement has to choose its battles. Legendary lawman Elliott Ness spent years trying to bust Al Capone for murder and organized crime, but he couldn't do it. Prosecutors eventually put Capone away for tax evasion. Ness felt as though he failed. I visited Capone's prison cell in Alcatraz and can testify it was sufficient punishment, no matter what the charge was. A conviction for tax evasion isn't as gratifying as a conviction for murder, but it did the job.

Your battles may not be as serious as law and order. Choosing them wisely will still have a huge impact on your effectiveness as manager. So how do you decide which battles you need to win? Start by asking these three questions:

1. How much will this matter in five days?
2. How much will this matter in five months?
3. How much will this matter in five years?

Your decision will become much easier after answering these questions.

## Be Specific

Don't make statements that are too broad to back up. For example, no one can summarily say he likes or dislikes surprises. Everyone likes surprises when they're good and hates surprises when they're bad. Ask the next person who says she hates surprises how upset she'd be if Ed McMahon showed up on her doorstep with a $10 million check. Conversely, the person who claims to love surprises won't be happy when he discovers his wife left him, his dog died, and his house burned down. You can specifically say, "I don't like surprise birthday parties" or "I do like surprise gifts." You cannot make broad generalizations.

An example managers face is the battle of bad attitudes. Never confront an employee by saying, "I need to talk to you about your attitude." The employee will automatically respond "What attitude? I don't have an attitude." You'll never convince him otherwise. The statement is too broad and too general to prove. You must be specific to win the battle. For example, pretend you own a restaurant and your bartender has a bad attitude. You should wait until you build a strong enough case to win before confronting him. Do this by equating the poor attitude to job performance. Confront him and say, "Three customers have complained that you were rude to them this week." Of course, he will deny it. He'll probably attempt to discredit the customers by saying they were wrong. Respond, "That was my first thought. This is why I didn't confront you after the first complaint. It was only an isolated incident and I gave you the benefit of the doubt. When I received the second complaint, it was a coincidence. I became a little concerned, but still gave you the benefit of the doubt. The third complaint clearly established a pattern of behavior. This is why we're discussing it now. This pattern of behavior is not acceptable in the food and beverage business."

## Baby Steps

This is all straightforward if you're managing a new team. But what happens when you've been managing the wrong way for years? Make changes in your company like you would make subtle adjustments with the steering wheel of a large SUV while flying down the interstate at 70 miles per hour. Jerking the wheel suddenly will cause the vehicle to overturn. Likewise, you don't want to drastically shift the direction of your company all at once. If you've allowed too much bad behavior to go on for too long, it will take some time to undo the damage. If you are patient, then you'll see results. The great thing about the human spirit is that people are incredibly adaptable. We don't like to change but we can when we have to.

Zig Ziglar told a story about an experiment conducted to see how well frogs could sense changes in temperature. The frog was first dropped into a pot of boiling water. He sensed the heat and immediately jumped out. He was next dropped into a pot of room temperature water. The temperature was turned up a few degrees at a time. He didn't notice the subtle change and stayed in the water as it boiled. Don't try to change everything in your company at once. Turn up the heat slowly. First, make a list of changes you wish to implement. Rank them by difficulty and how long you expect each to take. Don't fight the biggest or most important battle first. Instead, fight the easiest battle and get a quick victory under your belt. Your first goal is to build confidence in yourself, and nothing does this as quickly as winning a battle. It feels good to win, and you need to remind yourself that you can do it. The next goal is to build momentum. Your confidence level will soar when you win your second battle, and the momentum will carry you on to the next.

## Understand the Difference between Control and Authority

It's important to understand your own limitations. Having authority over an employee doesn't mean you have control over a situation. The registrar at my seminars always tells people to finish calls and turn their cell phones off before entering the room. There is a large sign on the registration table and another on the stage reminding them. I'm amazed at how many people disregard three notices and whip out their phones as soon as they enter the room. They assume it's okay to use the phone until the seminar starts. They believe they can end the call at exactly nine o'clock when I start speaking. They don't realize that they lack control over the situation. Have you ever tried to get someone off the phone quickly? The people in my seminar can't just press the END button when I tell them to stop talking. The person on the other end of the conversation may not be ready to hang up.

The other problem is that cell phone usage is as contagious as yawning. One person using his cell phone sends a message to others that it's okay for them to use theirs. By nine o'clock, there may be 100 people in the seminar with 15 still on the phone. If I ask everyone to hang up immediately, at least two will still be on the phone 10 minutes later. Ninety-eight people will then be ready to choke the two rude individuals who think it's more important for one person to hear them than for 100 people to hear me. I have authority, but only have limited control of the situation. Because I know what will happen at nine o'clock, I have to take action. I immediately tell people they'll have to leave the room as soon as they pull out their cell phones, even if the seminar doesn't start for another half hour.

Managers must know their limits. You can't change someone's character, make an unpleasant person pleasant, or make a person care. You can only set boundaries, reward the good behavior, and punish the bad. When people refuse to play along, they'll be ejected from the game.

## Understand the Difference between Leadership, Supervision, and Management

Managers often ask if they need to be at work at eight o'clock when everyone else arrives. They feel like it's their prerogative to enjoy some flextime, especially when they worked late the night before. Managers have added privileges because they have added responsibilities. The question is not if the manager has the right to come in later than employees, but whether it's wise to do so. The answer lies in whether you are a leader, manager, supervisor, or all three.

People follow leaders voluntarily. Therefore, leaders don't need formal authority over the people they lead; they merely need influence. For example, Martin Luther King Jr. was a leader. He had influence over the people who chose to follow him although he had no authority over them. He could not fire a follower or evict someone from the civil rights movement.

A manager must have authority over the people he manages. He is responsible for results and the buck stops with him. The president of your company has authority over you even though you may never meet him. He can fire any employee he chooses. Full-fledged managers have the authority to terminate employees. Those who don't are weak-armed managers. This is nothing derogatory toward the manager; it simply means someone above him is tying one arm behind his back by preventing him from doing what sometimes needs to be done.

A supervisor directly oversees the daily activity of others. This is a hands-on role. He must be physically present for maximum effectiveness. It's possible to supervise employees from a distance, but not advisable. Supervisors don't need the authority to terminate employees in order to be true supervisors.

Managers have the option of coming in later than employees. It's best if a supervisor is present in the manager's absence, but it is not always a necessity.

## Avoid Battered Manager Syndrome

Not even the problem employees would argue about whether management is a stressful job. Never underestimate the toll stress can take. According to Dr. Phil McGraw, parents of children with attention-deficit disorder (ADD) have three times the divorce rate of the general population.[2] Doctors have a much higher suicide rate than other professionals. The owner of a credit bureau in Louisiana told me the price he paid was quadruple-bypass surgery. A manager in Knoxville, Tennessee, told me she suffered two nervous breakdowns from work-related stress.

It seems like the United States is obsessed with syndromes. We now have everything from restless leg syndrome to hurried woman syndrome to irritable male syndrome. I am jumping into the fray with battered manager syndrome (BMS). Symptoms of BMS include:

- Dreading coming to work
- Feeling like you work for your employees
- Depression and anxiety when the weekend is over
- Hopelessness and feeling like you're always fighting a losing battle
- Loss of appetite, sleep, and sex drive
- An inexplicable desire to choke an employee

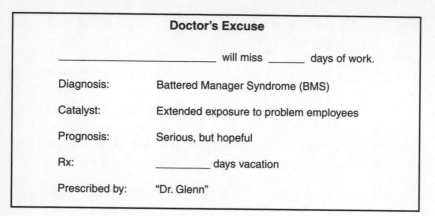

**Figure 2.1**   You may need to take a break.

Treatments include:

- Getting some victories under your belt
- Getting rid of dysfunctional employees who are contaminating the work environment
- Taking a vacation

Did you flinch at the last one? Have you not taken a vacation in years? If not, it's time for you to take a vacation. I am diagnosing you with BMS. You are hereby ordered to take a vacation (Figure 2.1).

## Conclusion

Prepare yourself before you attempt to solve the problems employees create. Taking an honest inventory of your own motivations, skills, and abilities comes first. Your own style and behavior influences everyone you manage. Strength is a necessity, and insincerity isn't acceptable. Choose your battles wisely, be specific, understand your own limitations, and don't take on too much too soon. Once you're sure you're up to the challenge of managing, make it as easy on yourself as possible. In the next chapter, we look at how to do this by creating an environment that minimizes problems for managers.

# CHAPTER 3

# Creating a Healthy Work Environment

**M**old and mildew grow in dark, dingy basements. Flowers bloom in sunny living rooms with plenty of windows. The work environment you create can foster cooperation and productivity or become a breeding ground for bitterness and hostility. Just as we use feng shei to arrange furniture in a room, there is an aura to every workplace. Healthy work environments don't grow by themselves. You must plant the seed and fertilize it constantly.

## Define Clear Boundaries

I receive e-mails every week from seminar attendees asking for my advice on situations ranging from employees eating at their desks to carrying guns to playing solitaire on the computer. My first response is, "What's your policy on this?" I never cease to be amazed how often the answer is, "We don't have one." We can't hold employees accountable for crossing boundaries unless we first define the boundaries. Employees are not mind readers.

Your values may seem reasonable and obvious to you, but don't assume everyone shares them. You must clearly communicate to your employees where the boundaries lie. It doesn't matter if employees disagree with the boundaries; it only matters that they respect them. Trust and respect are minimum requirements for any healthy adult relationship. Each person has to respect the boundaries the other has set, and must also be able to trust the other to respect his or her boundaries.

## Is Rebellion Always Bad?

If respecting my values requires other people to violate their own values, I can understand conscientious objection. If there's no sacrifice required, it becomes merely a choice. When one chooses not to recognize boundaries, then it becomes rebellion. Teenagers rebel indiscriminately because they're young. There's a proper time, place, and way for adults to rebel. There's also a time and place for complying. When adults don't understand this, they sabotage opportunities, relationships, and ultimately their futures. Martin Luther King Jr. encouraged people to protest civil rights violations, but always peacefully. He knew there was a right and wrong way to rebel. Natalie Maines of the Dixie Chicks learned this lesson in March 2003 when she publicly stated she was ashamed the president was from Texas. She did a mea culpa after fans reacted by boycotting concerts and radio stations pulled Dixie Chicks songs out of rotation. She said in a press statement, "I apologize to President Bush because my remark was disrespectful. I feel that whoever holds that office should be treated with the utmost respect."

It wasn't an issue of whether she had the right to criticize President Bush. Criticizing a president is certainly nothing new. The issue was the place, time, and way she went about it. She was in England during a time of war. Millions of English citizens were hostile toward Prime Minister Tony Blair and the United States for our involvement in Iraq. Our solders were already in danger. The last thing these soldiers needed was an American celebrity fanning the flames of anti-American sentiment. Comedian Robin Williams was smarter than Maines. Though he opposed the war in Iraq and frequently mocked President Bush during the election, he went on three USO tours to entertain the troops abroad. When asked by a reporter why he didn't criticize the president in his monologues, he responded, "Politics has no place on this tour. You want to debate? That's for home. Here, we concentrate on the soldiers. It's all for them." I saw Williams perform in Nashville in 2002 and concluded he was much smarter than most people realize. His remarks on the USO tour confirmed my conclusion.

Adults don't get to blurt out whatever they want to say, whenever and wherever they want to say it. There are places and times when we forfeit some of our personal liberties. You give up the right to carry a pocketknife when you get on a plane. You also forfeit your right to free speech. Just mention the word "bomb" and see how quickly federal agents will explain your rights to you. You also give up certain rights to be an American citizen. While you generally have freedom of speech, you can't even mention assassinating a U.S. president. Work is another place where people forfeit certain liberties. Employees give up the right to dress any way they choose, say anything they feel like saying, and behave any way they choose to behave. They are paid to respect the boundaries while at work.

## Set the Tone for Your Company

A good place to start planting seeds for a healthy work environment is with basic office etiquette. I constantly hear people ask what happened to good manners. Society has lost its social graces and bad manners surround us. It would be nice if everyone had good manners. It would also be nice to live in a perfect world. Neither is the case. Complaining about bad manners does nothing to correct the situation, especially for people who've never learned good manners. The question we must ask is not why people have bad manners, but how to get people to behave in a reasonably polite manner that is conducive to a healthy work environment. Begin with some basic groundwork. Create rules of etiquette and have each employee sign them. These are not policies and are not likely to be the sole cause for termination. They are simply values you expect people to recognize. The following is a sample list I compiled from pet peeves managers have shared with me:

*Rules of Etiquette in Our Office*

- Cover your mouth when yawning or coughing.
- Cover your nose when sneezing.
- Refill the paper or toner in the copy machine after using the last of either.
- Unjam the copier when it becomes jammed.
- Clean up after eating lunch in the breakroom.
- Refill the ice trays in the freezer after emptying them.
- Refill toilet paper or paper towels after using the last of either.
- Return all messages.
- Flush the toilet after each use.
- Put dirty dishes in the dishwasher.
- Show up on time for meetings.
- Do not tell off-color jokes.
- Do not speak ill of the company.
- Do not blow your nose while at the lunch table.
- Do not camp out in other employees' offices during business hours.
- Do not chew gum by smacking, constantly blowing bubbles, or not closing your mouth.
- Do not clip your nails at your desk.
- Do not discuss other people's wages or personal lives.
- Do not do any political campaigning.
- Do not enter an office without knocking, or open the door and knock as you enter.
- Do not hum to yourself.
- Do not interrupt someone who is having a conversation with a coworker.
- Do not loiter in another employee's office while he or she is trying to work.

- Do not look through faxes, take yours and leave the rest in a mess.
- Do not speak so loudly that everyone else can hear.
- Do not talk with food in your mouth.
- Do not interrupt others.
- Do not use others' phones when you have a cold.
- Do not use profanity.
- Do not e-mail someone who's in the same office when a personal word will do.
- Do not steal other employee's food from the refrigerator.
- Do not wear strong perfume or have strong body odor.
- Do not whistle.
- Do not answer your personal cell phone while in conversation with another person.

This accomplishes more than preventing the specific situations addressed in these rules. It sets the tone and communicates your leadership style. It also offers a benefit in the recruiting process. Give applicants a copy of your rules of office etiquette and ask if they would have a problem conforming to this atmosphere. Good employees who have worked in chaotic companies will flock to you because they'll want to work in a pleasant atmosphere. Those who object will reveal their true selves by doing so.

## We're People Bound by a Paycheck

Most new hires have the predisposition to be good or bad employees, but have the potential to go either way. Managers sabotage their chances of turning a marginal new hire into a top performer when we fail to clearly communicate what's expected and what won't be tolerated. Be realistic. Some managers take it too far by painting pie-in-the-sky pictures of what the employee can expect. Have you ever heard a manager say, "We're all one big, happy family at this company?" This is not true for five reasons:

1. People can't choose their families but can choose the company they work for.
2. People can't easily leave families but can easily leave a company by quitting or simply not showing up for work again.
3. Families can't easily force members to leave against their will but companies can force employees to leave at any time, without prior notice, and without cause.
4. Families can't choose who joins them but companies can choose their employees.
5. Many families today are dysfunctional. Your company is not.

If you're not convinced that you and your employees are bound only by a paycheck, think back to a time when either you or a coworker left the company. The two of you developed a friendship you thought would last forever, but lost touch after one of you left. You were hurt because you thought the relationship was more than it was. It was two people bound by a paycheck. Once the common paycheck ended, the bond no longer existed.

## Use Mentors to Instill Good Work Habits in New Employees

You have already set the tone for behavior; now it's time to set the tone for performance. None of us knows what our true potential is until we reach it. We tend to see our present level as the most we can do and best we can be. This is why it's important to set the bar high for new employees. New hires will form their own standards for quality and quantity of work within the first few weeks. Practice does not make perfect: It makes permanent. An employee who learns to perform a task the wrong way is likely to continue performing that task the wrong way. The more he practices, the more deeply engrained bad habits become. Intervene before bad habits are formed. Employees are most receptive to training when they're new; so spend as much time as possible with a new hire during this incubation phase. It's during this special time that he should be taught job skills, work habits, and work pace. Old habits die hard, whether good or bad.

Create good, strong habits in new employees before bad employees have a chance to influence them.

If it's not possible for you to personally train the employee, use a mentor who is a trusted nonmanagerial employee. A peer will be less intimidating than a manager, and the new hire will open up more. If your chosen employee doesn't want to be a mentor, try appealing to his or her pride. Say "I came to you because you're the best, and I want this new employee to learn from the best." Another option is to offer your chosen mentor a bonus. This is a perfect situation where money could be an ideal short-term motivator. You could also offer nonmonetary incentives such as time off. A seminar attendee in Georgia told me Frito-Lay gives drivers a Friday off if they'll spend Monday through Thursday training a new driver. You could also offer the incentive of using the new employee to do the mentor's work for a couple of weeks. Say to the mentor, "I want you to show the new hire how to do the job. As soon as he's up and running, all you have to do is watch him while he does the work." The mentor often holds the new employee to a higher standard than management can. If the new hire is struggling, he may think your standard is unreasonable. If it comes from a coworker who meets the standard, he's more likely to believe he can do it, too. Even if he doesn't achieve the higher standard, he'll still be well trained when the bar is set high.

## Use a Camcorder to Re-create the Hawthorne Effect

General Electric (GE) commissioned a study at a Cicero, Illinois, light bulb plant in the late 1920s. They wanted to determine if increasing the lighting sped up production. They informed workers they were installing additional lighting to determine this. The lighting was increased and workers also increased their output. Pleased with the findings, experimenters informed workers they were installing even more lighting to see what would happen. Lighting was increased again and workers increased their output again. For a brief moment it seemed as if GE would be able to sell an unlimited quantity of light bulbs to businesses by promising that additional lighting would increase productivity. This hypothesis was short-lived; subsequent tests revealed that productivity increased even when employees were told the lighting would be increased but experimenters did nothing. The lesson learned was that behavior changes when people *believe* they are being monitored.

Consider using a camcorder if you don't have an employee who can mentor during the training period. Videotape the employee for a day and have him watch the tape. Ask him to make a list of three things he did well and three things he would like to improve. I used this on new sales representatives years ago to critique their sales presentations. They were always their own worst critics. Their performance improved faster when they critiqued themselves than when I critiqued them. I experience this today when my seminars are taped. I'm a producer's worst nightmare because I hold myself to standards higher than anyone else holds me.

## The Importance of Dress Code

One simple way to set boundaries is with your company dress code. It's more critical today than ever before. Young men today show up for job interviews wearing shorts and muscle shirts. Others look like they just crawled out of bed wearing baggy jeans pulled down to reveal their boxer shorts, a baseball cap turned sideways, and three-day stubble. Young women show up wearing miniskirts and sandals. Others wear low-rise jeans, flip flops, spaghetti strap tops with no bra, and expose their midriff. Both genders further adorn their look with unlimited tattoos and facial piercings.

Managers ask me where it will stop. It will stop where you make it stop. You must decide what is appropriate, but it's not an easy decision. Organizations struggle with this nationwide. While churches and restaurants are loosening their dress codes, other establishments are tightening theirs. The Burger King in Cave City, Kentucky, makes their employees remove all facial piercings when they clock in. Prohibiting facial piercings is a yes-or-no proposition. Dress code becomes a murkier issue when trying to specify wardrobe dos and don'ts. Defining "business casual" for women is a nightmare. Fiserv Solutions in Jacksonville, Florida, offered the best solution I've seen. They went through dozens of magazines and clipped out pictures of women's fashion styles. They then pasted the photos on poster boards that they displayed in their breakroom. One board is labeled "No" and the other is labeled "Yes." Go to www.glennshepard.com/dresscode to view the dress code boards.

The key to making a dress code work is to keep it updated. Both public and private sectors are forced to constantly update their policies to keep up with social and technical trends. The U.S. Marine Corps updated its uniform regulations in 1996 to prohibit tattoos on the neck and head. The U.S. Army updated its policies in 2002 to authorize the wearing of pagers and cell phones for official army business. The U.S. Air Force updated its policy on body piercing in 2003 to prohibit body mutilation. The U.S. Navy updated its policy on pagers in 2004 to allow sailors to wear personal digital assistants (PDAs) and cell phones for official navy business. The new policy also allows female sailors to wear pants for official duty or even formal events. All branches of the military now have policies that require members to remove objectionable tattoos at their own expense. Failure to do so may result in punishment up to involuntary separation.

The Walt Disney Company in Orlando, Florida, loosened its dress code in 2000 to allow moustaches. They loosened it again in 2003 to allow women to wear hoop earrings as long as they are no larger than a dime. They allow only one ring per ear, which must be worn at the bottom of the ear. Post earrings are allowed as long as they are no larger than a quarter. Women may wear open-toe and open-heel shoes, but hosiery is required. Men are allowed to wear braids in their hair as long as they are above the collar. Men are not allowed to wear Oxford style shirts.

The change in generations makes the dress code even more important. Generation X is highly independent and known for being nonconformist. They came of age when flannel and earthiness was trendy. They may show up with body parts fully covered, but with wet hair and no makeup. They believe the au natural look is wholesome. Generation Next's values are quite different from those of Generation X. Generation Next values conformity, but their fashions are often so outrageous that they don't know how to dress appropriately for work. Seminar attendees constantly ask me about young women baring their midriffs. This is a result of Generation Next being raised to include everyone, accept everything, and expecting to be unconditionally accepted, so they let it all hang out. They haven't learned that they have to accommodate the employer, not the other way around. They're accustomed to society, including overindulgent parents, accommodating them. A dress code brings uniformity to as many as four generations who have to adapt to the same standard long enough to earn a paycheck.

## Conclusion

You can prevent a great deal of bad behavior by being proactive. It is your responsibility to create a healthy work environment. This includes defining hard boundaries as well as setting the general tone with issues such as etiquette and dress code. It is also your responsibility to set new employees up to succeed. This includes providing solid training and setting the standards high, while remaining realistic. Each minute spent helping a new employee acclimate to your corporate culture can pay back dividends in preventing problem behavior for years to come.

Now that you've taken steps to create a healthy work environment in your organization, you need to know how to staff it with the healthiest people. In the next chapter, we look at how to avoid hiring the wrong employees.

# How Do I Avoid Hiring Problem Employees?

**Y**ou have prepared yourself to be the best manager you can be. You have created a healthy work environment and set the tone. Now you need to know how to hire, who to hire, and where to find applicants.

## Don't Hire People You Intend to Fix

Never buy a home that needs significant repair unless you're in the home remodeling business. Home repairs always take twice as long and cost three times more than expected. Homebuyers with house fever invariably find that perfect little Victorian house or Cape Cod cottage in need of just a little tender loving care. Their financing has been preapproved, they're tired of shopping, their emotions overcome their good judgment, and they buy it. It can quickly become a not-so-funny adaptation of the Tom Hanks and Shelley Long movie

*The Money Pit.* Six months later, when the end is nowhere in sight, they're asking themselves, "What were we thinking?" Then the perfect little Georgian house comes on the market at the same price with no repairs needed. It stays on the market forever as a painful reminder of the price they paid for their impatience.

Managers encounter a similar situation when we have a job opening we need to fill. We know we should keep shopping until we find a good fit. However, we get tired of interviewing and grow impatient, become scared we'll never find a good hire, lose hope, and eventually become desperate. We end up at the point where we'll hire anyone who will just show up for the interview. Six months after hiring the employee we're asking ourselves, "What was I thinking?" You'll always regret decisions you make when you're:

- Angry
- Desperate
- Hopeless
- Hungry
- Impatient
- Scared
- Sick
- Tired and weak

This is not a time to become reckless. You're not in the people-fixing business. You're not a healer, life skills coach, or miracle worker: You're a manager. A good rule in life is not to marry someone you intend to change or hire people you intend to fix. Keep interviewing until you find a person who fits the job.

## What Are the Choices?

Four generations make up today's labor pool. The exact years of when each generation begins and ends are topics of debate. While the dates vary slightly, the values are fairly consistent. These are only trends and there will be exceptions to each. Yet, the trends have such a strong impact on motivation and work ethic that managers should be aware of them.

## The Silent Generation

The Silent Generation was born between 1925 and 1946. They're mostly retired now. They valued duty, discipline, delay of gratification, sacrifice, conformity, and were loyal to their employers. They expected to stay in one job and one marriage for a lifetime. Most of them came of age before the government got into the business of supporting people. Social programs such as unemployment benefits and Social Security were new. Labor laws such as the ADA and FMLA were half a century away. The Silent Generation had only two options: work or don't eat. Hence, they developed an extremely strong work ethic. Their exit from the workforce is a great loss for employers.

## The Baby Boomers

The Baby Boomers were born between 1946 and 1964 and number approximately 75 million. They had great optimism. Earlier members of this generation were largely responsible for the civil rights movement, the drug culture, and the sexual revolution of the 1960s. Divorce became socially acceptable for Baby Boomers. They are generally viewed as self-absorbed and egocentric. They rebelled against conventional family life and valued self-gratification and doing their own thing. Baby Boomers became yuppies in the 1980s when material wealth and status were the goals, and it was considered a virtue to work long hours. Their reliance on self-help products for everything from codependency to career success launched an entire industry. Baby boomer managers can be positive to the point of being annoying. They have a tendency not to accept blame and like being the star of the show. They're often perceived as controlling by Generation Xers, who value independence. The first wave of Baby Boomers are just beginning to exit the workforce.

## Generation X

Generation X was born between 1964 and 1982. At an estimated 19 million, it's much smaller than the generations that immediately preceded or followed. It's referred to as the lost generation because of its association with having an identity crisis. Generation Xers are politically nonideological and were shaped by the nonconformist grunge movement. They rejected the status, money, and social climbing that

Baby Boomers value. They're cynical, distrust institutions, and hate labels. They embrace risk and see themselves as free agents in the job market. They're independent thinkers who are sometimes viewed as arrogant or disloyal. Though often considered slackers, they were largely responsible for the dot-com revolution. They believe work should be fun, and place a higher value on time outside the office than Baby Boomers do. They now place a high priority on parenting. Generation Xers can seem aloof, lack interpersonal skills in the workplace, and dislike meetings and team focus. They don't value work for the work itself, are rarely workaholics, and often resent working after normal hours.

## Generation Next

Generation Next was born between 1982 and 1995. This generation is also known as Generation Y, the Millenials, or the Echo Boomers. Their parents are mostly Baby Boomers. Generation Nexters are nearly 80 million strong and are just beginning to enter the workforce. Their values are quite different from Generation X; Generation Nexters wish to conform and are far less independent. They're accustomed to being rewarded more for participation than achievement. They grew up being graded on how well they got along with others as well as how they performed academically. They're the most inclusive and tolerant generation ever; group thinking is the norm. Violent crime, smoking, drinking, and teen pregnancy have dropped substantially for this generation.

Generation Nexters believe they're all special because their parents' lives revolved around them. While their grandparents told stories of walking to school in the snow, they were chauffeured in SUVs and minivans from school to various after-school activities; they've been heavily programmed. Most Generation Nexters have never ridden in a car without wearing a seatbelt or ridden a bicycle without wearing a helmet. They grew up with computers, cell phones, and video games, and expect immediate gratification. Instead of shopping at the mall, they shop online and have whatever they order shipped overnight by FedEx. They're more accustomed to downloading their favorite songs off the Internet than buying a CD. They're the ultimate I-want-it-now generation and are used to getting it now.

One benefit to employers is that Generation Nexters should be less insubordinate and have more of a team-player mentality. Another could be their materialism. Money and the rewards a job can bring were less meaningful to Generation X, which was highly idealistic and less materialistic. Generation Nexters' materialism might make it easier for employers to find rewards and incentives to offer. Employers of young Generation Nexters have already discovered that rewards such as Apple iPODs or Sony Play Stations can be easy carrots to dangle for good performance.

Negative characteristics will include a lack of individuality and initiative. Nexters are so conditioned to being continually entertained by television, DVD players in cars, and handheld video games that they don't know how to entertain themselves. Highly imaginative pastimes such as hide-and-seek or cops-and-robbers are foreign to them. The price they have paid for their technical literacy is loss of imagination and creativity; they're used to having someone think for them. Competing to excel in the workplace will be a difficult transition since they've been conditioned to fit in. They expect life to be like a video game; their thinking is very short term and delayed gratification is a foreign concept. They aren't risk takers. They also expect you to tell them how wonderful they are without achieving anything.

## Decide What You're Looking for in an Employee

A common mistake managers make is failing to first define what they're looking for in an employee. To avoid hiring problem employees, you must understand what to look for and what to avoid. You should look further than whether an employee is stable or dependable. Some basic qualities should apply to all employees; others won't be a matter of right or wrong as much as making sure the applicant's personality fits the position. Some employees are good with people but lousy with details. Others are great with tasks but lack people skills. One frustrated manager described a customer service representative by saying, "He doesn't understand that he has to be polite. He just says things in a way that makes people want to hurt him." In order to find the best fit, you should answer some basic questions about the position before you evaluate applicants to fill it. Is speed (i.e., harvesting a crop before it goes bad) or accuracy (i.e., checking punctuation in a million dollar contract) more important? Will this employee be working independently (i.e., a toll-booth worker) or on a team (i.e., on a production line)? Should this employee like the public (i.e., retail) or prefer working in a non-public environment (i.e., data entry)? If interacting with customers, would he or she prefer phone work (i.e., taking catalog orders) or face-to-face interaction (i.e., a cellular phone store)? If she likes the public, should it be orderly (i.e., a seminar) or raucous (i.e., a nightclub)?

Your company also has a personality, and the applicant's personality should fit your company's. Maybe your employees are loud and energetic. Although this seems fun to you; it may seem boisterous and disorderly to others. Maybe your employees are quiet and orderly. This may seem efficient and appropriate to you, but boring and monotonous to others. The most dangerous driver on the road is not the speed demon who comes roaring by you at 100 miles per hour. It's not the little old lady who is doing 30 miles per hour. The most dangerous driver is the one who's going 40 miles per hour when everyone else is going 70, or going 70 when everyone else is going 40. Drivers can do either legally. Practically, one must conform to a group of people in order to fit in with the group. Don't hire applicants who won't fit your company's personality.

## How Many Employees Should I Hire?

Because business is cyclical, customer demand will never exactly equal the supply of labor. Consequently, businesses go through periods of being slightly overstaffed or understaffed. The lesser of the two evils is to be slightly understaffed. Having too much to do and too few employees to get it done forces us to be more resourceful. This is when people rise to the occasion. It's no problem getting people to relax when things slow down again. Having too many employees and not enough work creates lazy, bored, and unmotivated employees. It's a huge challenge to get employees who are accustomed to producing 80 units a day to crank it up to 100, even if 100 units was always the quota. Employees who slack off will become habitual slackers; it's human nature to resist being asked to produce more.

Note that I am referring to being slightly understaffed, not critically understaffed. We wouldn't want three people trying to run an entire Wal-Mart store on Christmas Eve. This would create a critical shortage of labor and would be disastrous. Staffing needs change by the season, the day, and even the hour. Listen closely the next time you're in a restaurant or retail store that's nearly empty. You're likely to hear the manager asking for volunteers to clock out and go home. Managers have this flexibility when paying on an hourly basis. We lose this flexibility when paying a flat salary. For example, your phones might ring off the hook Monday mornings, but are dead on Friday afternoons. If your staff is salaried, you're throwing money out the window each Friday afternoon by paying them to answer nonexistent calls. When in doubt, it's better to not hire enough employees than to hire too many.

## Where Do I Find Good People to Hire?

I'm amazed at how many people whine about not being able to find work but won't work at finding a job. They expect a job to find them. They think the perfect job should appear out of thin air as soon as they open the newspaper or go online, and are surprised when it doesn't. Going door-to-door to look for employment is a foreign concept to them. It never occurred to them that companies may have job openings they haven't yet advertised. It also hasn't occurred to them that companies may consider creating new positions if the right applicant came along. They just don't get it. They're too lazy to get out there and make it happen but still complain that there are no jobs.

On the other side of the equation are lazy employers who expect job applicants to find them. They whine that they can't find good people to hire but won't do anything about it. We already established in Chapter 1 that many people don't want to work. Even those who do aren't exactly hustling to find employment; you must find them.

Running ads in the newspapers or on the Internet won't cut it any more. Broaden your horizons on your prospective labor pool.

Not every potential employee is mailing out resumes. Some are gainfully employed and aren't actively looking for another position. If the right job came along, however, they'd change jobs in a heartbeat. The good part about a workforce with no sense of loyalty is that it's easy to hire people away from other companies. Hiring a new employee is like getting married. The interview process is the dating phase, the probationary period is the honeymoon, and termination is like a divorce. There is one major difference between marriage and employment: When looking for a spouse, you don't date someone who is presently married. This isn't the case in employment. There's nothing unethical about courting employees who are currently working for other companies. They're not married to the company, so everyone is fair game.

Other potential employees aren't even in the job market right now. They have left and are considering reentering it. Retirees, recent widows and widowers, stay-at-home moms and dads, people whose spouses have suddenly become unable to work, people who returned to college later in life, the recently divorced, and even people who are thinking about divorcing may become potential employees in the near future.

Finally, remember that most people don't stay in the same industry their entire careers. Bank tellers go to work in veterinary practices. Dental hygienists become insurance sales representatives. Plumbers become truck drivers. This means you're competing with every employer in virtually every industry. You must get creative to attract labor.

## Always Be Recruiting

The conventional labor sources that worked well a decade ago aren't working now. Employers have to look at unconventional methods and sources. Remember that by creating a healthy work environment and being a strong manager, you'll make your company an attractive place to work. We'll look at unconventional sources for labor in the following section.

## Canvass the Neighborhood

One fringe benefit employees put on the top of their wish list is a short commute to work. A manager in Pennsylvania told me she posted job openings in the laundry rooms of nearby apartment complexes. She even stapled flyers on telephone poles and drew considerable walk-in traffic. This guerilla recruiting method is not limited to small businesses. I was recently handed a flyer announcing job openings while walking through the parking lot at a Wal-Mart store. What made this unique was that the company handing out the flyers wasn't Wal-Mart, it was United Parcel Service (UPS). UPS is known for paying well. Yet, even they have to get out there and hustle to find good employees. If you think this is too unprofessional for your company, I have one question for you. Do you want to whine about the lack of job applicants or get out there and get the job done? If UPS has to work this hard to find people, so do you. Remember that you're competing with virtually every employer out there. The company that works hardest to find applicants is the one who finds the most.

## Churches

Call the pastors at every church or synagogue within walking distance of your company. Speak to the head pastor, assistant pastor, minister of music, church secretary, youth pastor, and anyone else who will talk to you. Tell them you're looking to hire. Pastors are a direct link to hundreds and sometimes thousands of potential employees. They're also in the unique position of knowing personal details about people's lives. They know when parishioners might be interested in working but aren't actively looking. Perhaps a church member is struggling financially. Some churches even have a job board. It's free and there are usually no legal restrictions such as those employers encounter when advertising in the newspaper.

## College Students

The American Council on Education estimates that 80 percent of college students work 20 hours per week or more. If you're near a college campus, call the placement office and ask if they have a job board. Also ask about internships. Some college majors require students to intern in an industry affiliated with their major. The students receive class credit and some even work without pay. You will experience lower turnover because college credits are tied to performance. You may also be able to hire the intern full-time after graduation.

## Create a Resume Pool

Have you ever kept a gift you didn't like and later given it as a gift to someone else? One creative manager took this approach with resumes. She asked applicants if they'd like her to pass their resumes on to other companies in the event she hired someone else. Most were more than anxious for her to do this. Each time she filled a position, she walked through her office building distributing the remaining resumes. When she had an open position, she went knocking on doors, asking for resumes in return. The practice became like a bartering system: "I'll trade you one secretary looking for $28,000 a year for two sales representatives willing to work on commission." Because the pay scale, timing of job openings, and requirements differed, she rarely found her company competing head-to-head with the other businesses for the same individuals.

## Every Employee Must Help Recruit

Bankers have to open new accounts. Sales representatives have to bring in new leads. Parents sell candy for their child's school fundraisers. Churches and civic organizations expect members to recruit. Add to everyone's job description that they're expected to be nonstop recruiting machines. Pay for them to join the Chamber of Commerce, Kiwanis Club, Toastmasters International, alumni associations, and any other organization where they can network. Have your employees recruit everywhere they go. Give an employee a Friday afternoon off to play golf. Tell him that if he brings in the name and number of a potential hire, you'll pay for his next round of golf.

Offer your employees bonuses for bringing in new hires. One financial services company pays $1,000 to the referring employee as soon as the new hire reaches six months. Another pays $500 after 30 days and the remainder after six months. Even small amounts can work. One company gives business cards to all its employees and pays $20 each time they bring in someone who fills out a job application. If you can't afford to pay, give an extra day off for employees who bring in an applicant to interview. Every employee is a headhunter for your company.

## Mystery Shop

Restaurant chains employ mystery shoppers to eat at their various locations. Since servers don't know that the customer is also an employee, the mystery shopper gets a candid image of the employee's performance. This is not only used to catch problems, but it also catches employees doing things well. Many employees have been promoted because a mystery shopper observed stellar performance.

You and your employees can become mystery shoppers as well. Every employee of every hotel, car dealership, doctor's office, restaurant, department store, body shop, garage, hair salon, gas station, bank, and any other business you patronize is a potential employee for your company. Carry business cards with you at all times. When you encounter people who take pride in what they do, write your personal cell phone number on the back of your card and hand it to them. Tear a $20 bill in half, giving them one half and keeping the other. Tell these potential employees you're looking for good people and would like to talk to them about coming to work for you. The other half of the $20 bill is theirs if they will come in and fill out a job application. Allow them to call on your personal cell phone after hours so that they don't jeopardize their present job.

## Former Employees

Consider contacting former employees and asking if they might be interested in returning. One major accounting firm mails surveys to former employees three months after they leave and asks if they would consider returning. They rehired close to 1,000 former employees in one year. Employees who have left you may have found out that the grass wasn't greener on the other side of the fence, but are too embarrassed to call because they think you wouldn't welcome them back.

## High-School Students

Federal labor law allows children as young as 14 years old to legally work under certain restrictions. High-school students are members of Generation Next, which means less insubordination and rebellion. This could be the best time in years to hire high-school students. A McDonald's in Baton Rouge, Louisiana, gives raises according to the student's report card. The better the student's grades, the higher the raise. Tying compensation to grades produces several benefits. It reduces turnover because the student has to wait until report cards are issued to get the raise. It also helps with recruiting efforts because straight-A students know other straight-A students.

## Hire from Your Competitors

The owner of an air conditioning and heating company asked how he could mystery shop when his business isn't retail. He could place a service call to one of his competitors and observe the technician who responds. By simply unplugging a wire or shutting off a gas valve at his house, he can test a potential employee's technical skills as well as his customer service skills. He could find the perfect employee for the cost of a $35 service call. He could also have his employees take turns sitting at home and calling technicians. Some people ask if this is ethical. Yes, it's ethical; it's free enterprise and it's survival of the fittest. Companies compete to hire employees just like they compete for customers.

Hiller Plumbing in Nashville takes their recruiting effort even further. They want to hire experienced plumbers and work hard to attract them. They recently ran the following ad in a local newspaper:

Are you a plumbing service technician? If so, let's talk! I have a great job opening for which you might qualify. I am looking for a service tech who would enjoy above-average pay, a 40-hour plus work week, year round work, super benefits, and (here's the part you will like) a $4,000 signing bonus and maid service for one year FREE! Now, this job isn't for everyone. We are the best in town, so only the best should apply. Must have a good attitude and like working with people. Heck, I'll even give dinner for two at Applebee's and two passes to a Regal Cinema theater for any bona fide person who fills out an application. So dinner and a movie are on me.

## Hire from Your Customers

Hiring from customers scares some business owners, but it shouldn't. They fear they'll lose a customer if they try to recruit the customer's employees. This doesn't have to be the case. If you sell to other businesses, simply inform the employees you deal with that you are looking to hire. Ask if they know someone who might be interested. Remember that the average job lasts about three years, and most of your customer's employees will eventually leave anyway. There are also economic realities. If your customer pays its employees $8 an hour and you pay $14 an hour, it would be unrealistic for them to expect their employees to pass up a 75 percent pay increase.

## Hire from Your Vendors

Hiring from vendors is easier than hiring from your customers. You are the customer, so your vendor is unlikely to cut you off if you hire its employee. You also have the added benefit of having already seen how an individual follows through, handles crises, and generally does his or her job. Tell each of your existing employees to inform every vendor they deal with that you are hiring.

## Inmates

Nearly 80,000 inmates currently hold jobs in the government or private sector. A warden who attended my seminar told me her inmates are screened and monitored so carefully that employers have essentially zero problems with insubordination. Inmates earn only minimum wage in many states, with 50 percent of their wages going to make restitution to the victims of their crimes and 25 percent directly to the inmate's family. Some companies build their businesses around this unique labor niche. U.S. Technologies in Marietta, Georgia, has operations in four prisons. A travel agency in New Boston, Texas, uses inmates to make travel reservations. It may not be the perfect option for you, but it is an option.

## Retirees

People are living longer than ever, and many are choosing to work past the traditional retirement age of 65. The outcome is different when someone works because he chooses to. One benefit is lower rates of unscheduled absenteeism. A 72-year-old employee will usually call in sick less often than a 32-year-old. These individuals are part of the Silent Generation, which values duty and discipline. They're loyal to their employers and are also stable. Unlike the twenty-something or thirty-something employees who are still trying to find themselves, retirees know who they are and where they want to be. If you want to experience firsthand a retiree who wants to work and enjoys it, just look at a Wal-Mart greeter.

## Split One Full-Time Position into Two Part-Time Positions

Instead of hiring one full-time employee, consider hiring two part-time employees. Their hours can be split so that you have 40 hours of continuous coverage in the position, which allows you to tap into sources of labor not interested in full-time employment. Hiring part-time employees also provides you with more flexibility. Let's go back to the distribution center example from Chapter 1. You need 120 hours of permanent labor per week. You could hire three full-time employees at $10 per hour and work them 40 hours per week. When you need extra hours, you have to pay the overtime rate of $15 per hour. Alternatively, you can hire four part-time employees at 30 hours per week. You now have four people who can give you up to 10 extra hours each week at their standard rate of pay.

## Soccer Moms (or Dads)

You may have a great source of part-time labor if your company allows part-time work during hours of the day when children are in school. Often parents have been out of the workforce a few years and have a desire to get back in to update their job skills. They generally have a high level of motivation. Many parents revolve their lives around their children. A person who is a parent first and wage earner second could be a prime source for labor if you can offer a flexible schedule.

## Temporary Agencies

Even though the hourly rate will be higher, temporary employees (temps) are often money well spent. Temporary agencies are a good way to "try before you buy." If you don't like the employee they send over, you can call and ask for a replacement. You can usually buy out the employee's contract from the agency when you find the right one. Owners of temp agencies in my seminars inform me it's common to waive buyout agreements for good customers.

Remember, always be recruiting!

# Screening before the Interview

Once you know what you're looking for and have a pool of applicants to choose from, you'll need to weed out the unacceptable applicants. An experienced manager can read a resume and immediately identify an undesirable candidate. Let's look at some red flags.

## Job Hopping

The average job lasts about three years. The average employee takes about six months to top the learning curve. At this rate, an average new hire will not begin to earn his paycheck until he's 15 percent of his way to leaving you. I don't want to waste 15 percent of an employee's tenure paying him to learn a skill that he won't stay long enough to use. The job hopper hasn't figured out what he wants to do when he grows up. One seminar attendee in Little Rock, Arkansas, called these "serial employees." Another asked, "Would you seriously consider marrying someone who has been divorced six times?" Job hoppers are unstable and will leave you as soon as they are trained. Don't waste your time and money on them.

## The Long-Term Employee

Most managers know to avoid hiring applicants with a history of instability, but many miss the opposite side of the coin. The applicant who was at his previous job for 18 years is stable, but could still be a bad hire. He's more likely to stick around but may be less receptive to training because he's been doing things the same way for years. I would never refuse to hire someone because he's stable; stability is what we want. I would simply look closely to see how flexible he is.

## Gaps in Employment History

An applicant has a stable employment history. She has been at her present job for three years, and was at her prior job for five years. She has a two-year gap between the jobs. This may not be a bad sign, but it does raise a question. You need to know what she was doing for those two years. Perhaps it was something perfectly legitimate. Perhaps it was something sinister. She might have gone back to school, been in an institution, been incarcerated, had a job she doesn't want you to know about, or spent time with her family. You need the missing piece of the puzzle in order to get a complete picture of the applicant.

## Compensation History

Smart managers avoid pay cuts when hiring. They also avoid giving disproportionately large pay increases. An individual actually has less motivation to work when his income suddenly jumps. Financial windfalls can wreak havoc, even when individuals are accustomed to having money. For example, look at Jack Whittaker of West Virginia. Few thought money would be a problem for him because he was already a self-made millionaire. Yet, his life fell apart after he won nearly $315 million in the lottery on Christmas Day 2002. He was arrested twice for drunk driving, sued by three women for molesting them at a racetrack, burglarized three times, arrested for hitting a bar manager, and ultimately attributed his granddaughter's death to the windfall of cash. One common consequence of employees receiving windfall pay increases is increased absenteeism. When people suddenly have more money than they need to make ends meet, they have less need to work. Pay increases are good; pay increases that create windfalls are not.

## Part-Time Employees versus Full-Time Employees

Don't hire an applicant who wants full-time employment if your opening is part-time. You'll only be a temporary employer while he looks for a full-time position. If you directly ask whether he's looking for full-time or part-time work, he'll say whatever he needs to say to get the job. To get the real truth, say, "This job is only part-time. If it were to go full-time later, would you be interested?" If he answers yes, you know full-time is what he's looking for now. If he says no, you may have a good fit.

## Screening during the Interview

Interviewing is an art. It's the art of trying to get an accurate read on a stranger's character, work ethic, dependability, and willingness to learn in about 30 minutes. Interviewing job applicants is similar to dating before marriage. People show their best side while dating. They'll say what you want them to say, dress like you want them to dress, and be on their best behavior. The real person then emerges after a few months of wedded bliss. Surprises come out in marriage even after years of dating. Likewise, it's next to impossible to get the whole story on a job applicant in 30 minutes.

Interviewing gives you power. The hand that rocks the cradle may rule the world, but the one that writes the checks controls it. You're making a decision that affects numerous lives in major ways when deciding who gets a job. It's a challenge to wield so much power prudently. To make the challenge even greater, we're all biased.

One tendency is to help people you believe are worthy of your help. Maybe you meet an elderly widow who reminds you of your mother and you hire her. Another bias is to hire people you find attractive, or not hire people you find unattractive. We all have biases based on appearances. One way of overcoming this is to conduct the first interview over the phone. This is a more efficient way of screening applicants quickly, plus the conversation can be recorded and played back later. This allows you to pick up subtle nuances you missed in the initial conversation, and you'll find yourself writing down more questions you would like to ask the applicant. Eleven states require the consent of both parties to record a conversation. Even if you live in a one-party consent state, always inform the applicant you will be recording. As long as he or she gives permission, it's perfectly legal in all states. In-person interviews can then be scheduled with those who sound most promising.

You'll need to look deeper once an applicant passes the initial screening. One method is to take the applicant to lunch or dinner and insist that his wife attend. Getting away from the office is a great way to get someone's true personality to emerge, especially for those who freeze up in a formal office interview. Watch how he treats his wife, as well as how he treats the server. Someone who's nice to you but rude to the server is not a nice person.

One manager in Toledo, Ohio, sends a spy out to the parking lot while the applicant is in the interview. This spy looks inside the applicant's car to see if it's a pigsty. I pointed out that my car sometimes looks like a pigsty. He explained that a messy car doesn't faze him, but when someone has beer cans, a spare tire, and old milk cartons in the back seat, he takes notice. He also asks his spy to inspect the car's exterior. He explained that whether the applicant drives a junker or brand new car doesn't reveal mounds of information about him. A relatively new car that has been bumped, dinged, backed into, dented, and has the shape of a phone pole in the bumper does. Employees who abuse company property or leave tools at job sites sometimes cost more than they earn. He reasoned that an applicant who doesn't take care of his automobile wouldn't take good care of a $2,000 company computer. His method certainly wasn't scientific, but it worked for him.

Regardless of your approach, it's important to learn as much about the applicant as possible. Next, let's look at some sample interview questions.

## What Are Your Strengths?

Applicants know how to give answers that sound good but really don't answer the question. For example, an applicant tells you she's a hard worker. This is nothing more than lip service. We expect every employee to be a hard worker. Can you imagine an applicant telling you she's lazy? Another applicant tells you he's honest. We expect everyone to be honest. Can you imagine an applicant telling you he's going to embezzle from your company? Another applicant tells you he's dependable. We expect everyone to be dependable. Can you imagine an applicant telling you he'll call in sick once a week? Require all applicants to explain their answers with specifics. For example, ask an applicant exactly what he means by being dependable. If he hasn't missed a day of work in 10 years, he moves to the top of the list. He drops to the bottom if he responds, "Well, uh, I just am." Some managers get so desperate for help that they nearly answer the questions for the applicant. Don't make that mistake.

## What Three Things Would You Change about Yourself If You Could?

This is the most important question. You know she has a realistic view of herself if she gives reasonable answers. She has a problem if she can't come up with a single answer. If she has such low self-esteem that she can't stand to critique herself, she certainly can't stand to hear it from you. She could become the passive employee who cries every time you correct her. She could become the passive-aggressive employee who pouts every time she's reprimanded and then calls in sick the next day. Knowing how much fallout there's going to be, you'll find yourself putting off correcting this problem employee. Then you'll have a bigger problem. If you don't correct someone's bad behavior, it will become more frequent and more severe. Then it will spread like a virus that infects every other employee. Don't hire applicants who won't acknowledge their own weaknesses.

## In What Areas Do You Feel Your Present Boss Could Do Better?

Many of us fought authority in our youth. Eventually most of us got past it. When an applicant critiques his present boss, you'll learn more about the applicant than about his boss. If an applicant responds, "My boss is the biggest jerk you've ever met," then he's still fighting authority. He'll be saying the same thing about you in six months.

## Why Do You Think You Would Fit in Here?

An applicant must have researched your company in order to answer this question. This is important because all jobs look easier from the outside. Dog lovers apply for jobs as veterinary assistants, thinking they'll get to play with puppies all day. They quit three days later when they realize they'll be spending much of their days cleaning out cages. Firefighters have a similar problem. Applicants are prepared to walk into a blazing inferno, but aren't prepared for the boredom between calls. The fire chief from a small town in Kentucky found a unique way of solving this problem. He schedules all interviews at 8:00 A.M. and makes applicants wait until 10:00 A.M. before he begins. His reasoning is that if they can't wait for an interview, then they can't wait for a fire. It's your responsibility to make sure the applicant knows what he's getting into before it's too late.

## Why Are You Leaving Your Present Job?

Be suspicious when someone answers "personality differences." We all have personality differences with coworkers. How we handle them reveals what kind of people we really are. Personality differences don't justify quitting a job unless there's more to the story. The applicant may have a problem getting along with other people.

## When Could You Start?

It's important to know what level of professionalism the applicant possesses. You want to hear two weeks if he's currently employed. If he'll walk out on his present employer with no advance notice, he'll do the same to you.

## If Hired, How Long Would You Stay?

Of course you'd like hear something like, "I wouldn't take a job unless I could see myself retiring with the company." I once asked a job candidate this question and she answered, "In three months I'll be leaving because my husband's in the military and being transferred to Connecticut for advance training." You'll get a direct answer if you ask a direct question. Don't assume anything.

## Tell Me Why You're the Right Person for This Job

This is not as obvious as it sounds. You'll be amazed at how many people will be stumped by this one. Make him sell himself. If he's not willing to work to get the job, he won't be willing to work once he's hired.

## Screening after the Interview

Completing the interview process doesn't mean the screening process is over. Smart managers continue screening applicants after the interview, to further weed out potentially bad hires. Let's look at some common methods for doing this.

### Credit Checks

Credit checks reveal more about a person than how well he pays his bills. Some insurance companies won't write or renew policies on individuals with bad credit or heavy debt because statistics show these customers are more likely to file claims. Federal prison guards in Georgia told me credit checks are run on them every year, and guards who accumulate too much debt or fall behind on paying their bills can lose their jobs. The government knows that guards in financial trouble are more likely to accept a bribe to look the other way when an inmate wants to attack another or smuggle in contraband. Many companies regularly run credit checks on employees who handle company funds for similar reasons. Some people insist they would never be tempted to embezzle no matter how bad their personal finances are. This is exactly why credit checks are smart. People who believe they're above temptation are the most susceptible to it. Rick Warren pointed out in *The Purpose Driven Life* (Zondervan, Grand Rapids, MI, 2002) that given the right circumstances, any of us are capable of giving in to temptation. Smart managers avoid putting an employee in a position that might be too tempting.

A low credit score doesn't systematically disqualify job applicants. Many successful business leaders failed before they succeeded. Walt Disney and Henry Ford filed for bankruptcy early in their careers. However, most people you interview aren't going to be great business tycoons. The credit score helps round out the picture of an applicant. Imagine that two identically qualified applicants are applying for the same position. One has a credit score of 300, which is the lowest possible. The other has an 850, which is the highest possible. Most companies will hire the applicant with an 850. How we handle money reveals much about our level of discipline, maturity, and self-control.

The Fair Credit Reporting Act requires that you notify a job applicant in writing on a separate document and get his or her written authorization to run a credit check. If the applicant asks why you're doing this, explain the reasons above. Contact your local credit bureau or go directly to the web sites for the three major credit bureaus at www.experian.com, www.equifax.com, or www.transunion.com.

## Criminal Background Checks

The United States now has over two million people in prison, more than any other country. Nearly one-fourth of those are incarcerated for drug-only offenses, and most will reenter the job market after being released. The reason for running criminal background checks is not necessarily to disqualify applicants who have served time. Some companies will still consider an applicant who served time for a nonviolent crime if he can convince them he would be an asset to the organization. He could actually offer two advantages. If he is on parole, he'll likely be required to keep gainful employment as a condition of parole. He also has a parole officer the manager can call if he is not pulling his weight. Second, he will have fewer jobs available to him. If other employers turned him down because of his conviction, he might be a little more motivated to keep a good job. The obvious downside is the recidivism rate. Depending on the offense, the chance of an ex-con committing another crime is substantial. The positive side is that ex-cons who are gainfully employed have a lower recidivism rate than those who are not. These are generalizations employers should take into consideration.

## Drug Screening

The statistics on the impact of drug usage in the workplace are overwhelming. Employees who abuse drugs cost their employers about twice as much in medical and workers' compensation claims as nonusers.[1] The National Cocaine Helpline of Summit, New Jersey, reports that 75 percent of callers admit to having used drugs on the job, 44 percent admit to having sold drugs to fellow employees, and 18 percent admit to stealing from their coworkers to pay for their drugs.[2] Drug testing applicants is a smart idea. Federal law does not allow employers to test applicants for drugs until a job offer has been extended. The offer should be conditional upon the applicant passing the test.

Talk to different testing labs about their methods. Some tests are more refined than others. A urinalysis is easy to beat. A user can pass the test by abstaining for a few days before. He can also buy adulterants to mask the drugs or buy clean urine over the Internet, complete with special devices to heat it to body temperature. Many businesses are now paying the higher cost for hair testing. Organizations from Blockbuster to the Federal Reserve use hair testing. The New York City Police Department detected 5 times as many drug users among recruits by using hair tests as it did with urinalysis, and 30 times as many with probationary officers. Hair testing at Boston's police department found 23 employees using drugs that urinalysis missed.

## Preemployment Tests

Preemployment testing has become a multimillion dollar industry. Employers can purchase aptitude tests, integrity tests, personality tests, psychological tests, and skills tests from countless web sites. Numerous state and federal legal restrictions on these tests can create legal minefields for employers. Lawsuits have been filed claiming multiple-choice aptitude tests are discriminatory toward minorities because they reflect the applicant's test-taking ability more than his job skills. Personality tests can violate the Civil Rights Act of 1964 by bringing up personal issues such as one's religious beliefs. Psychological testing can imply mental disorders and create violations of the Americans with Disabilities Act. Integrity tests are not expressly prohibited by federal law, but can violate privacy laws. The Federal Employee Polygraph Protection Act does not apply directly to integrity tests. However, it could serve as a precedent in arguing the legality of integrity testing. Still, preemployment tests can work when used properly. Speak with your attorney before using them.

## Ride Alongs

Some people are smooth as silk in interviews but become dead-weights as soon as they're hired. Many employers invite applicants to spend a day observing to see if they really want the job. An applicant for a sales position may ride with the sales manager while she calls on prospects. An applicant for a customer service position may spend a day in the call center. Seeing the applicant in the work environment can reveal more about her than how she acts in a sterile job interview. Spending a day together also gives the employer eight additional hours to observe the applicant before extending an offer.

## Conclusion

Knowing how to discern the right applicants from the wrong ones is a skill many managers spend decades trying to master, and still fail to do. Having an idea of who your ideal employee would be, what your choices are, and where to find applicants is the place to start. Once you've staffed as best you can, it's helpful to look at how to avoid creating problems with good employees by making bad decisions regarding money. In the next chapter, we look at how much impact compensation has on the workforce.

# CHAPTER 5

# Taming the Compensation Monster

**D**eciding how to properly compensate employees is an age-old dilemma for managers. Underpaying causes turnover to skyrocket while overpaying results in little motivation to improve and advance. The dollar figure is not as important as being competitive within the industry. Even in fields not known for high pay, employers must be competitive without being too generous. The Tennessee prison system is currently facing this dilemma. Over 600 of Tennessee's 2,431 prison guards left their jobs in 2004, mostly because of the low pay. Many were able to get substantially higher-paying jobs without leaving law enforcement. The starting salary for a deputy with the Davidson County Sheriff's Department in Nashville is just over $28,000. Starting salary for a state prison guard is just over $21,000. It comes as no surprise that Tennessee has the fourth highest turnover rate in the nation for prison guards. When employees can drive across town and get a job in the same industry paying

32 percent more, they're going to do it. On the other side of the dilemma was the assistant chief of a small town police department in the Midwest. Rookie officers didn't want to take routine calls or make traffic stops in cold weather. Typically, a young officer presents the opposite problem. Rookies are sometimes so overzealous that their superiors have to remind them not to write tickets to drivers going 56 miles per hour in a 55 mile-per-hour zone. They want to get more stripes on their sleeves and earn more pay. I asked why rookie officers in this department weren't anxious to advance. The answer floored everyone in the seminar; new officers in his department start off at $52,000 a year. They don't need promotions to pay the rent.

## Entitlements versus Incentives

Benefits that are given are called *entitlements*. They can't be earned because they require no effort on the recipient's part. Entitlements destroy a work ethic; people have no incentive to work for something they take for granted. Benefits that must be earned are *incentives*. They help build a work ethic. Employees only reap this benefit from hard work.

For example, cost-of-living adjustments (COLAs) are perks to keep employees' present wages stable in relation to inflation. If a company chooses to offer this perk, it becomes an entitlement. Therefore, COLAs offer no incentive for good performance.

Christmas bonuses also offer no incentive for good performance. All an employee has to do to earn a Christmas bonus is have a pulse on December 25. Hence, it is an entitlement. Replacing Christmas bonuses with year-end bonuses which are tied to performance makes them incentives. People who perform more earn more money.

## The Problem with Raises

A raise is not a reward for loyalty or past performance; it's a statement that the employer believes an employee will be worth more in the future. The employer is attempting to predict the employee's future behavior based on his past behavior. People who have never been in management sometimes ask, "Then what's my reward for 20 years of service to the company?" The answer is, "Twenty years of paychecks." The concept of working for money is a matter of unpaid accounts. If an employee works Monday through Friday this week and isn't paid until next week, the employer is indebted to him until then. The account is settled once this debt is paid. The employee works first to earn the money and the employer pays after the money has been earned. Raises work in the opposite direction. A raise is an opportunity and an obligation. The employee is now obligated to become more valuable to the company. His or her job becomes less secure because we expect more from him or her with each raise. This is why a company president who makes $2 million a year is more vulnerable to termination than his or her secretary who makes $28,000 a year.

Instead of basing raises on an individual employee's effort, some organizations give raises across the board. An entire department might receive a 3 percent raise regardless of individual performance. I meet thousands of managers in local, state, and federal government agencies who struggle with this. They have employees who want to do a good job, but are demoralized when slackers receive the same raise they do. Raises should be given according to individual performance.

## Seniority, Salary Creep, and Coasting

It is commonly assumed that employees are worth more the longer they stay. This is not always the case. An employee's value to an organization depends on his continued performance. Let's look at an example. We'll ignore inflation, benefits, and learning curves to keep this simple. Assume an employee was hired at $500 a week in 1995. He yielded $1,000 of average weekly productivity his first year. His net worth to the company (what he generated minus what he cost) was $500 per week.

### Scenario A

Ten years later, the employee still earns $500 per week and still yields $1,000 of average weekly productivity. His net worth to the company remains $500 per week.

## Scenario B

Ten years later, the employee still earns $500 per week but yields $2,000 of average weekly productivity. His net worth to the company is now $1,500 per week; three times what it was when he started. This increase in net worth has nothing to do with his tenure with the company; it's a result of his increased productivity. If he reached the $2,000 of average weekly productivity starting in year three, then he hasn't increased his net worth for the past seven years.

## Scenario C

Ten years later, the employee earns $1,500 per week and yields $2,000 of average weekly productivity. His net worth to the company remains $500 per week. Despite the fact that his average weekly productivity has doubled, his net worth is exactly where it was 10 years ago because his salary has crept up over the years.

## Scenario D

Ten years later, the employee earns $2,000 a week and yields $4,000 of average weekly productivity. His net worth is now $2,000 per week. Even though his salary has quadrupled, his production has as well. Assuming the employee doesn't present behavior problems, he has the closest thing there is to true job security (although it could later hurt the employer legally if the manager said this out loud).

## Scenario E

Ten years later, the employee earns $1,700 a week and yields $2,000 of weekly productivity. His net worth is now $300 per week. Despite the fact that his productivity has doubled, he's worth less now than when he was hired 10 years ago. His productivity didn't keep up with his salary creep.

Scenario A and B are not realistic. No one will make the same salary 10 years later. The employee will fall under one of the last three scenarios. Scenario C is acceptable, scenario D is desirable, but scenario E is an unfortunate reality for many. People slack off and try to coast when they take their jobs for granted. This is why the doctrine of employment-at-will works.

Another problem with raises is that they can back an employer in to a corner. Give too much of a raise and you won't be able to afford more in the future. This is what happened to an attorney named Ben. Ben hired a paralegal at $8 an hour. He gave a $5-an-hour raise after one year, putting the paralegal at $13 an hour. She asked for $8-an-hour raise the next year. He couldn't afford it and lost the employee, despite offering a $4-an-hour increase.

## When Employees Ask for a Raise

Don't chastise an employee asking for a raise. Ask the employee to explain why he or she deserves it. Use it as an opportunity when he or she responds, "Because I can't make ends meet on what I'm making now." Ask, "Why do you think I give raises? Is it based on each employee's individual needs, or each employee's individual productivity? I want you to get the raise. I'm even going to help you because you've taken the initiative. How much of a raise do you want? Name your price. Your raise will become effective when you become more effective. Now tell me what you're going to do to make yourself worth that amount."

## The Tennessee Titans Face a Tough Management Decision

Salary caps in professional sports force coaches and managers to deal with salary creep in a painful way. The coaches and management of my beloved hometown football team faced this dilemma at the beginning of the 2004 season. Heisman Award winning running back Eddie George led the Titans in rushing for eight years. He also led the team off the field with countless appearances for charity and community events. The music of Nashville was squelched at each home game by chants of, "Eddie, Eddie, Eddie" from a stadium full of fans who worshipped him. He was one of the most popular players in Titans/Oilers history, but was also one of the most expensive. His base salary in 2003 was $5 million. He played in all 16 games of the season but broke 100 yards rushing in only 2. Meanwhile, a young rookie named Chris Brown came on strong. Despite limited playing time, he gained 221 yards to George's 1,031. He also made only $230,000. George's salary was over 21 times more than Brown's. In other words, George's rushing cost almost $4,850 per yard while Brown's cost about $1,040 per yard. Head Coach Jeff Fisher and General Manager Floyd Reese made one of the most difficult decisions managers can make. It was also one of the smartest. They let George go and elevated Brown to the starting running back position. Brown rushed for 100 yards or more in six of the seven games he played in 2004. George was traded to the Dallas Cowboys. The decision would have been easy if he was one of those high maintenance prima donnas, but he wasn't. The Titans' attorney who provided me with this data wrote in a postscript:

> You should know that our organization has immense respect for Eddie George and what he accomplished during his tenure as a Titan. Despite the fact that he is no longer our player, we wish him nothing but success in his future endeavors. He will always be considered among our greatest all-time players. (personal correspondence)

I suspect Titans management and coaching staff endured a sleepless night or two before arriving at this difficult decision. Yet they did what they had to do.

Salary caps, which are actually a payroll limit for the entire team, are a double-edged sword. They force coaches to make sacrifices in order to stay under the cap. Players know their future with the team becomes more uncertain as they shoot up the salary structure. Show business poses a different dilemma. Actors can ask for as much as they want since there are no salary caps. Actors also know they can't easily be replaced. Ray Romano's salary was $800,000 per episode when he entered his eighth season of *Everybody Loves Raymond* in 2003. Kelsey Grammer had just ended his 11-year run on *Frasier* at $1,600,000 per episode. After tense negotiations, Romano signed a contract paying him about $1,800,000 per episode. You can ask for a 125 percent raise when you're the star of the number one show on television. But rest assured you have created an obligation to remain the number one show. Salary creep can become your worst enemy.

## The Ideal Compensation Plan

The ideal compensation plan is to pay the lowest wage base throughout the year and the highest year-end bonus possible. This offers three major benefits to the employer. First, it decreases overtime costs. Let's look at two examples where an employee makes $30,000 a year:

### Example 1

An employee's total annual compensation is $30,000. His hourly rate is $10. He earns a $20,800 base and gets a $9,200 bonus at the end of the year. His overtime rate will be $15 an hour if his employer needs him to work extra hours. His overtime rate is $5 per hour more than his standard rate.

### Example 2

The same employee is compensated totally on an hourly basis. His hourly rate would be approximately $14.43. His overtime rate jumps to $21.65. His overtime rate is $7.22 per hour more than his standard rate. This is an additional $2.22 per hour, or 44 percent more than the overtime premium of $5 per hour in example one.

The second advantage of large year-end bonuses is reduced turnover. If an employee gets an attractive job offer in September, he'll be more hesitant about leaving his present job since he already has eight months invested in the year-end bonus. I personally know this to be the case because the employee I just described was myself. When I left corporate America on September 1, 1988, I had to really think about it. I knew I was walking away from a year-end bonus I had invested eight months into earning.

The third benefit is that a substantial part of the employee's compensation is now tied to performance. The bonus should be based on the company's performance and the individual's contribution. Any employee can contribute by bringing in new hires. Another way to contribute is to suggest ways to save money. You'll see the result of this each time you stay in a hotel room. Years ago, a housekeeper at a hotel in Orlando, Florida, suggested her company could save money by not changing bed sheets every day. Hotels everywhere now save thousands of dollars and millions of gallons of water each year by changing bed sheets only when requested or after guests check out. Employees can also earn year-end bonuses by selling back unused sick time, which is discussed further in Chapter 8.

## Will Bonuses Cause Friction between Employees?

Managers sometimes ask me if awarding different bonuses might cause jealousy between employees, or worse. My answer is "absolutely!" If bonuses are commensurate with performance, the underperforming employee will receive less. He will not be happy about this. If bonuses are the same for everyone, the employee who gives 110 percent will be unhappy that the slacker received the same thing. The question managers should ask themselves is "Which employee do I want to be unhappy?" A good rule to implement is, "anyone who whines or complains loses his bonus next year."

## Conclusion

While money is not a primary long-term motivator, poorly structured compensation packages will demotivate employees. Money will also heavily impact your ability to attract and keep good employees. Even if you don't have the authority to set compensation, it's still beneficial to examine your company's compensation package to determine if it helps or hurts your efforts to manage. It is also crucial for managers to ensure that employees understand the obligations and increased expectations that accompany raises. In the next chapter, we examine what many consider to be the biggest nemesis of management today—the legal system.

# CHAPTER 6

# How to Avoid
# Legal Pitfalls

The United States is the most litigious country in the world. Even cartoon characters aren't immune to the problem. Brazilian tourism officials threatened legal action against the Fox Network after an episode of *The Simpsons* showed Homer being kidnapped and mugged in Rio de Janeiro. Employers are now the juicy targets. Many people have decided it's easier to get money from employers by suing them than by earning a paycheck. Nothing you or your lawyer can do will prevent it altogether. However, you can take steps to reduce the chances of litigation and limit your exposure. The following steps are not a substitute for consulting a good attorney. However, it would be smart to discuss each of these issues with him or her.

## Consider Having Employees Agree to Binding Arbitration

Alternative dispute resolution (ADR) exploded in the United States after a 1991 U.S. Supreme Court ruling held that employers could require employees to settle statutory claims for employment related disputes, such as for discrimination, using arbitration.[1] In ADR, disputes are settled by an arbitrator or a panel of arbitrators who are often retired judges. It's a simplified version of a trial. Potential pros for employers include the following:

- Arbitration is usually faster than going to court.
- Decisions are confidential.
- Decisions are usually final, with no appellate rights.
- Financial awards can be less than in jury trials, depending on jurisdiction.
- Attorneys usually aren't involved.
- The process is less expensive.
- There is no discovery, which means no depositions.
- Simplified rules of evidence allow employers to bring up relevant issues in an employee's past.

However, arbitration is not a panacea for employers. It also has potential cons. Those include:

- Easier access to arbitration than to the court system could allow more employees to bring claims.
- It's difficult to overturn unfavorable decisions.
- Potentially damaging hearsay is allowed.
- Arbitrators who focus on equity instead of law may try to appease both sides by compromising between the parties, even when an employee is clearly wrong.

Despite the potential cons, the potential pros of arbitration are substantial enough to merit consideration and discussion with your attorney. If he or she decides arbitration is right for you, it must be set up carefully if it is to be enforceable. Arbitration has become the latest target of court assaults on employment-at-will. In 1999, a federal court in South Carolina refused to compel an employee to submit her sexual harassment claim to arbitration, despite having signed an arbitration agreement.[2] In 2002, the U.S. Supreme Court ruled that the EEOC could sue an employer for an ADA claim, even though the employee signed an agreement to arbitrate.[3] In 2004, a federal court in Philadelphia ruled that arbitration agreements a large insurance company required its employees to sign were unenforceable.[4]

Despite the court's assault on ADR, it remains a widely used tool. The agreement to arbitrate ideally should be signed at the time of hiring. Many companies include it in the job application. The following is an example:

> Because of the delay and expense of the court system, [Company] and I agree to use confidential binding arbitration, instead of going to court, for any claims that arise between me and [Company]. Without limitation, such claims would include any concerning compensation, employment (including, but not limited to, any claims concerning sexual harassment or discrimination), or termination of employment. Before arbitration, I agree first to present any such claims to [Company], to complete any [Company] internal review process, and complete any external administrative remedy such as with the EEOC. In any arbitration, the then prevailing employment dispute resolution rules of the American Arbitration Association will apply.

Don't attempt to set up an arbitration agreement on your own. Because of the recent legal challenges, it is critical that you have a good attorney set it up for you. Contact the American Arbitration Association at (212) 716-5800 or www.adr.org for details.

## Consult with a Good Attorney before Problems Occur

I'm amazed at how many people open a business and consult an attorney on whether to set up shop as an S Corp, C Corp, LLC, LLP, PC, or sole proprietorship, but never ask about personnel issues. Invest some time in talking with an attorney who specializes in labor law *before* you need one. Have her review your application for employment, disciplinary forms, employment-at-will statement, job descriptions, and policy manual. She can also brief you on recent changes in labor laws and recent court decisions that set new precedents.

## Have Employees Confirm Employment-at-Will Status

Clearly document the employment-at-will relationship in writing and have employees sign the document. As with the agreement to arbitrate, this can be included in the job application. The following is an example:

> I understand and agree that if employed, the employment will be "at will." That is, either I or [Company] may end the employment relationship at any time, for any reason, or for no reason. I understand that employee handbooks, manuals, personnel policies, and procedures at [Company] do not imply contracts of employment, and do not modify my employment-at-will status.

## Reiterate Your Right to Change Terms of Employment at Any Time

The doctrine of employment-at-will means there's no guarantee of future employment. It also means there is no guarantee the present terms of employment will remain the same. The employer has the right to decrease wages, hours, and benefits. From a practical standpoint, employers rarely do this except when absolutely necessary. You will sometimes hear about a large company such as an airline asking for voluntary wage concessions in order to stay solvent. They must ask because the collective bargaining agreement prohibits them from making changes without the labor union's consent. Employers-at-will generally don't have to ask permission to make such changes. Your employees may be able to draw partial unemployment benefits if you decrease their hours; this is better than going out of business. The most common example is increasing co-pays or employees' share of health insurance premiums. The changes are unpopular, but employers don't have to ask permission to make them. Spell out on the job application that you retain the right to change the terms of employment at any time. The following is an example:

I further agree that I do not have an employment contract and that my employment can be modified at any time by [Company].

## Using Misrepresentations and Omissions to Your Advantage

In an online survey conducted by the Society for Human Resource Management, 55 percent of the respondents said they found inaccuracies on resumes.[5] Dr. Wayne Ford, author of *How to Spot a Phony Resume,* says that some employers estimate over 60 percent of resumes to be phony.[6] Because the same problem exists with job applications, state on the application that any misrepresentations or omissions by the applicant will be grounds for termination. The following is an example:

> In completing this application, I understand it is very important that I be completely truthful, and that [Company] is relying on my truthfulness. I agree that if it should be discovered that the information I am providing is inaccurate, misleading, or incomplete in any respect, I will be disqualified for employment. If I have already been hired, my employment will be terminated immediately and I will forfeit all related benefits.

## Get Permission and Release of Liability to Run Background Checks

A 1997 revision of the Fair Credit Reporting Act requires that employers get permission from job applicants to run certain background checks. Even if only asking for information from references provided by the applicant, it's still smart to have the applicant sign a statement releasing you from liability. The following is an example:

> I authorize the references listed on this application to give you any and all information concerning my previous employment and pertinent information they may have, personal or otherwise, and release all parties from all liability for any damage that may result from furnishing this information to you.

## Employment Practices Liability Insurance

Insurance companies such as Chubb and State Farm began offering Employment Practices Liability Insurance (EPLI) policies in the 1990s. EPLI protects companies against lawsuits for discrimination, harassment, and wrongful termination. Premiums usually cost less than responding to a lawsuit that never makes it to court. Ask your insurance agent about EPLI.

## Hire on Probation

Smart employers start new hires out on probation. Even though employers-at-will can terminate at any time, it's easier to do so when an employee is still on probation. Probation is a period during which somebody's suitability for a job is being tested. During probation, employees must prove themselves to the employer, and can normally be terminated with no right to appeal the termination. Even in civil service jobs, employees on probation don't have the same right to due process as permanent civil service employees. While most employers use a 90-day probationary period, this is not enough time to get an accurate picture of most people. The FBI has one of the most thorough preemployment screening processes of any organization in the world. New recruits go through an extensive battery of tests and background checks. Despite this, the FBI realizes they can't get a full picture of an employee in 90 days. Their probationary period is one year. Even Montana, which is not an employment-at-will state, specified a six-month probationary period in its 2001 amendment to the Montana Wrongful Discharge Act. In order to better weed out problem employees, consider extending your probationary period to six months.

Probation is an excellent tool for management. However, it could also backfire. Attorneys representing employees in wrongful termination lawsuits have used the fact that an employee was fired shortly after probation ended to argue the employer didn't act in good faith. For this reason, some employers have changed the term from probation to "vesting period" or "orientation period." Talk to your attorney about this.

## Limit Conversations at Termination

Conversations at termination should be short and to the point. When you get to this stage, there's nothing left to discuss. You already held numerous discussions with the problem employee in the process of progressive discipline. Letting the conversation drag out now could result in two undesirable outcomes: You could either change your mind or say something that can later be used against you. Labor lawyers summarize it, "The more you say, the more you'll pay." It's too late to discuss the issue now. If the employee asks why he's being fired, respond, "I didn't fire you. You fired yourself!"

## Secure a Release of Claims When Terminating an Employee

Now that I've recommended you consult an attorney regarding your employment practices, let's look at how smart attorneys protect themselves when firing potentially litigious employees. They have the employee sign a general release of claims against the firm in exchange for severance pay. This is a *quid pro quo* situation. Quid pro quo is a Latin term that roughly interprets as "Do this to get that." To create a lawful quid pro quo situation, there must be consideration, which is usually money. The employer is buying protection. Ask your attorney to draft such an agreement before you need it.

## Don't Provide References on Former Employees

Even after you make a clean break with an employee you can still be sued. If you're asked for a reference on a former employee, it's legally prudent not to give one; tell anyone who asks that you have a policy against giving references. If you give a bad reference, there is potential for a defamation suit. Even if your former employee admits the negative information you reported is accurate, he could still file an action against you based on tortuous interference. Your truthful words prevented him from obtaining employment elsewhere. Even if you gave a good reference on a good employee, the new employer could have a cause of action against you if the employee doesn't live up to the reference you gave. The dates of employment are the only safe information to give.

## Protect Yourself from False Claims of Racism and Sexism

Falsely accusing a manager of racism or sexual harassment is one of the nastiest things employees can do. When dealing with either, you look guilty by association and lose the presumption of innocence. Thomas Jefferson wrote in the *Declaration of Independence* that all men are created equal and endowed by their Creator with certain inalienable rights. I believe in what Jefferson wrote. All employees should be treated equally. No one should be treated differently because of his or her skin color or gender.

However, a manager is not automatically sexist for disciplining a female employee or racist for disciplining a minority employee. I have met thousands of managers who were afraid to discipline a female employee because she threatens to claim sexual harassment or a minority employee because he or she threatens to claim racial discrimination. In our efforts to right the past wrongs of racial intolerance and women being treated as second-class citizens, we have now created a dangerous situation. Employees who have not suffered discrimination can exploit hypersensitivity to these issues and perpetrate extortion. This is a travesty for both the manager who becomes impotent to manage and the real victims of discrimination.

## How Bad Is Sexual Harassment?

Employees who experience true sexual harassment can suffer serious consequences. I met a woman at my seminar in Decatur, Illinois, who gave a deposition in one of the most atrocious cases of sexual harassment in U.S. history. She was previously employed at the Mitsubishi plant in Normal, Illinois, where male coworkers routinely groped women. Some women claimed they were forced to agree to sex to win jobs. Sketches of genitals, breasts, and various sexual acts were drawn on car fenders labeled with female workers' names and sent down the assembly line. Off-site sex parties were held and photographs were distributed around the breakroom. One woman found the door of her home bashed in and a note in her locker that read, "Die Bitch!" The plant's human resources director came home one night to discover his house burned to the ground. After a three-year investigation by the EEOC, Mitsubishi entered into a consent decree to pay $34 million to the victims.

For a female employee who is written up for being tardy to equate her warning to what happened at the Mitsubishi plant is ludicrous. Yet, it happens every day. Employers are terrified at the thought of going through an investigation with the EEOC or a state agency. The cost of legal representation can be so overwhelming that innocence or guilt becomes irrelevant.

Even when an employer is guilty, employees can exploit claims of sexual harassment. For example, in late 2004, a producer for *The O'Reilly Factor* filed a $60 million lawsuit against host Bill O'Reilly and the companies involved with his show. If Mr. O'Reilly said what she accused him of saying, he would be guilty of sexual harassment. Because I was not there and don't know what really happened, I will not pass judgment. For the sake of this discussion, let's assume he was guilty as accused. According to the U.S. Department of Labor's web site (www.dol.gov) state workers' compensation laws list of benefits, a worker who loses an arm at work in New York would qualify for a maximum of $124,800. The producer sued for $60 million because of a conversation. Is it wrong if Mr. O'Reilly said these things to an employee? Yes. Did she suffer because of his words? Maybe. Is she entitled to over 480 times what she would have received if she lost an arm? No!

## Playing the Race Card

Equally bad is being accused of racial discrimination. This is currently the most sensitive hot button in employment law. Due to the long and often violent struggle of the civil rights movement, Americans are more sensitive to racial discrimination than gender discrimination.

Our hypersensitivity to racism can be even more easily exploited than sexual harassment. I have met numerous White managers who are reluctant to reprimand an African American employee because he or she has threatened to file a racial discrimination complaint with the EEOC. This scenario is not limited to White supervisors and African American employees. I also meet African American managers who are confronted with the same threat from White employees. Recently, I encountered the most unusual racial discrimination case of my career. An African American employee at a manufacturing facility claimed racial discrimination by an African American supervisor. The employee claimed racial discrimination due to color variances in skin tone between himself and his supervisor. The case was eventually dismissed but only after thousands of dollars were spent on legal fees. So how does a manager discipline employees who make false accusations of racial discrimination or sexual harassment? You must be fair and consistent in your dealings with all employees, and you must be able to prove it.

Understand that you face an uphill battle in that the burden of proof is overwhelming. Anyone accused of a crime in the United States is presumed to be innocent until proven guilty. The prosecutor must meet the burden of proof in proving the guilt of the defendant. There are four basic levels of burden of proof in our justice system. The highest is *beyond a reasonable doubt,* which is used in criminal trials. The next highest is *preponderance of the evidence,* which is used in civil trials. The next is *clear and convincing evidence,* which is used in child custody cases. The lowest standard is *probable cause,* which is all a police officer needs to pull you over. These standards apply in a court of law where rules are rigorously enforced by a judge. They benefit prosecutors, defense attorneys, plaintiffs, and defendants by clarifying the rules. Managers do not have this benefit. As any manager who has ever fought a claim for unemployment benefits or a lawsuit for wrongful termination will tell you, the employer is presumed to be guilty until proven innocent. The burden of proof for the employer is:

> Be able to prove beyond the shadow of a modicum of an atom of an iota of a doubt that you have done nothing wrong.

The only way to meet this burden of proof is to practice the three cardinal rules of management: "Document, document, document."

## Conclusion

Completing this chapter won't make you an attorney, but it does place you above the majority of managers in your basic legal knowledge. You are now better equipped to spot and avoid some of the legal pitfalls that plague managers everywhere. Now that you have a rudimentary working knowledge of labor laws, we look at some basics of behavioral psychology in the next chapter.

# CHAPTER 7

# Why People Do the Things They Do

To handle problem employees, it helps to understand why they do the things they do. We all have the choice of being good or bad. Bad behavior is more contagious than good behavior. It's more fun to be bad because it allows immediate gratification, gives in to impulses, and requires no discipline. Being good requires delaying gratification; having self-control, discipline, and all those things none of us like. People will be bad unless there is a punishment for being bad or a reward for being good. The cardinal rule of behavioral modification is to reward good behavior and punish bad behavior. The difficulty lies in figuring out the best way to do this because it's different for each person. What is sheer terror for one person is sheer exhilaration for another. Because it is so difficult to find the right rewards and punishments, we sometimes get them backward. We accidentally reward the bad behavior and punish the good behavior.

## If You Loved Me, You Would Buy This for Me

The challenges of parenting provide excellent metaphors for the challenges of management. I witnessed a prime example of a parent rewarding bad behavior at a toy store in Georgia. A young mother was shopping with her daughter, who was about six. The little girl had the biggest blue eyes I've ever seen and knew how to use them to her advantage. She took a doll off the shelf, tilted her head to the side, and flashed those baby blues. In her most innocent angel voice, she said, "Mommy, I want this doll." Her mother said, "No. It's not your birthday and it's not Christmas. Put it back. If you're a good girl, maybe Santa Claus will bring it for you this year." When the charm failed, the little girl decided to try negotiating. She said, "Mommy, I really, really, really want this doll. If you'll buy it for me now, it can be my Christmas present and my birthday present." Mom turned and said, "What part of no don't you understand? I said put it back!" After negotiating failed, the little girl decided to try manipulation. She whined, "If you loved me, you would buy this for me." Mom responded, "I'm going to take my belt off and show you how much I love you." When the manipulation failed, the little girl pulled out the sure-fire winner. She threw a temper tantrum. She screamed, stomped her feet, and cried, "Mommy, you don't love me any more! You don't like little girls. If I was a boy, you'd buy me a G.I. Joe." The screaming caused quite a scene. Mom was embarrassed as people gathered to see what this cruel woman was doing to her innocent little angel. In her moment of embarrassment, Mom grabbed the doll and shoved it in her daughter's hands, yelling, "Here, take the stupid thing and shut up!" Mom just taught her little girl how to get what she wants. Do you know what's going to happen to that little girl 20 years from now? She's going to grow up and come to work for you. Perhaps she's already working for you. It is now your job to teach her the lesson her mother didn't.

It's easy to second-guess this mother's parenting skills, but managers make similar mistakes with employees. Imagine that you gave your problem employee verbal and written warnings. You then gave him a three-day unpaid suspension. This was supposed to be a punishment, but he came back with a suntan. He didn't get punished; he got a vacation. This becomes even more ridiculous when suspending an employee for absenteeism.

## The Pain of Being Bad Must Outweigh the Pleasure

You are on a diet and go to dinner with a friend at Outback Steakhouse. Your diet only allows a salad for this particular meal. Your friend orders a Bloomin' Onion that the server places right in the center of the table. You feast on a glass of water while your friend devours those batter-dipped, deep-fried onion slices. Next come the entrees. While your friend enjoys the medium-well Outback Special, you pick croutons off your salad and lust for honey mustard dressing, which is not on your diet. Next comes dessert. While your friend attacks a Chocolate Thunder from Down Under, you enjoy a boring cup of decaf coffee. You salivate as you watch the server clean the next table and wonder why someone would leave half a slice of cheesecake uneaten. Why didn't you plow into the Bloomin' Onion, Outback Special, or Chocolate Thunder from Down Under? It would have been indescribable pleasure, but only temporarily. Long after the pleasure in your tummy subsided, the consequences would show on your waistline. The punishment would be your avoidance of full-length mirrors every time you get out of the shower. Your present discipline will pay off in the future when you actually have a desire to look at yourself in the mirror instead of avoiding it. Everything we do is out of the desire for pleasure or the avoidance of pain. The pleasure of the meal you forfeited was tempting. The pain of the consequences won out, albeit by a narrow margin. To change an employee's bad behavior, we must make sure the pain of the punishment outweighs the pleasure of being bad. Let's look at four basic models in behavioral psychology to lay the foundation for changing this behavior.

## The Passive Individual

Passive people want to be liked. They love for people to pity them, and they fear all types of conflict. They'll do anything to avoid conflict. Some of the methods they employ include:

- Becoming a hypochondriac
- Becoming a people pleaser
- Becoming a "yes" man or woman
- Becoming apology-aholics
- Being indecisive and wishy-washy
- Crying
- Developing a victim mentality to elicit sympathy from others
- Giving away power
- Trying to create guilt in anyone who holds them accountable
- Using money to buy love

Their skills in manipulating situations are the stuff of legends. When confronting a passive person about his or her bad behavior, you're likely to hear childlike responses such as:

All you ever do is criticize. You never notice the things I do well.

Don't I do anything right?

If I'm such a horrible employee, why don't you fire me?

I didn't think what I did was that bad.

I only did it once.

I thought you were my friend.

I'm doing my best, but it's obviously not good enough for you.

No one appreciates all the good I do around here.

That's not fair.

While the responses differ, notice the consistent theme is to minimize the significance of the bad behavior. The passive individual is attempting to shift the focus away from what he or she has done. The payoff for being passive is the avoidance of accountability. Passive people can't be blamed for anything because they're not in control. Everything happens *to* them. The consequences of employing passive people are numerous. Passive people don't take initiative because taking initiative increases the chance of failure. They fear failure because it could create confrontation. A passive employee does not want to risk doing something that could result in a lecture from the boss about being irresponsible. Passive people are not risk takers, and therefore accomplish less than other employees. They have poor problem-solving skills, relying on others to solve their problems for them. They'll agree to anything but often drop the ball. They won't make decisions when tough decisions must be made.

The key to managing passive employees is to hold their feet to the fire. Managers need to hold all employees accountable, but the need is even stronger with passive people who have built their lives around avoiding blame. Let's look at an example.

One method passive people use to wiggle out of reprimand is to respond, "You're being mean to me." Passive people thrive on powerlessness. Teach them empowerment by giving the following speech:

No, I'm holding you accountable. Screaming, "Get off your rear end and get to work, you lazy maggot!" would be mean. Someone who doesn't care about your well-being might say this. I care. This is why I would not sit idly and watch you drive off from our Christmas party after you had too much to drink. I would not sit idly while you did drugs. I would not sit idly watching while you developed a gambling addiction. Caring means holding people accountable for their behavior. Your attempt to avoid accountability by blaming the messenger for the message tells me you may not have had many people in your life who have cared enough to take time to do this. I have invested in your success and I believe in you. You and I are going to succeed together. Now here are my questions for you: Do you believe in yourself? If so, what do you think I want to accomplish by holding you accountable for your own behavior?

No matter how much passive employees try to wiggle out of being held accountable, don't let them do it. If you're unsure of how to respond to their attempt to avoid accountability, simply say, "Has that actually worked for you in the past? It's not going to work with me."

Remember, this is a tough love approach to management. This benefits their personal growth and development as well as their professional growth and development.

## The Aggressive Individual

A passive person avoids accountability by getting you to feel sympathy. An aggressive person avoids accountability by getting you to feel fear. Aggressive people try to intimidate because they want to be feared, not liked. Passive people cry when reprimanded, while aggressive people yell. Despite opposite approaches, the goal is the same. Each wants you to back off. Don't do it. Never reward bad behavior unless you want more bad behavior in the future.

### Who's the Alpha Dog?

It is often said that a man's best friend is his dog, and there is good reason for this. Men behave similarly to dogs. The most important role in the dog world is the alpha dog, which is the top dog. Imagine two 100-pound male rottweilers meeting for the first time in your backyard. They will immediately size each other up to determine who will be the alpha dog. They'll sniff each other out, growl, and urinate in the grass. They'll then back down more often than engage in a dogfight. This means each has sized up the other and concluded he can't win. Even dogs know it's better to call a truce and walk away than fight a battle that can't be won.

This same scenario happens in the human species. If you have two sons, you have witnessed this from the day your second son was born. They will spend their lives competing with each other for alpha dog status. Even when they're grown, you'll relive the old days every time your family reunites for the holidays. I experienced this firsthand a few Thanksgivings ago when I found myself taking two little boys to see the Harry Potter movie. We didn't even make it into the car before the first fistfight erupted. It was over who was riding in the front seat. That was an easy solution. I put them both in the back seat, foolishly thinking I had the situation under control. We got exactly two blocks down the street when I made the mistake of taking a turn a little too sharply. The seven-year-old leaned over and touched the nine-year-old. The second fistfight erupted in less than

60 seconds. I turned around and explained there was to be no hitting or touching—or there would be no Harry Potter. As we happily sojourned along, I heard the nine-year-old say to the seven-year-old, "What are you looking at, Butthead?" Those boys were going to find a way to posture for alpha dog status even if they couldn't touch each other.

### Defense Implies Guilt

The good part about dealing with aggressive employees is that everything is out in the open. Let's look at an example:

Warren, a supervisor, asks Sluggo to perform a reasonable task. Sluggo responds with, "Why do I have to do it? You never make George or Michelle do it." Warren now has an employee who is challenging his authority. How would you respond? Answers managers give include:

- Because I said so!
- You're the best person for the job.
- George and Michelle are busy.
- Why don't you want to do it?

The problem with each of these is that defense implies guilt. If Warren defends himself to his employee, he gives away authority. Sluggo has no right to question why he has to do something reasonable; he is being insubordinate. To add insult to injury, he brought George and Michelle into it. What other employees are, or are not doing, is irrelevant. Warren can't afford to answer the question because he rewards the bad behavior if he does. Instead, he should respond: "That's an inappropriate question." This accomplishes two goals simultaneously. First, Warren doesn't allow himself to be put on the defensive. Second, Warren is defining a boundary by telling Sluggo that he doesn't get to ask the question again in the future.

### Don't Negotiate with Terrorists

A female optometrist who attended my seminar in Virginia faced a moment of truth with her aggressive employees. She had three employees who were all women. She worked in what she described as a "hormone-rich environment." One of her employees was the trouble child who did everything wrong. The two good employees resented the problem employee getting away with so much. One day the optometrist caught her problem employee doing something so egregious that it could have caused her to lose her license, so she fired the employee. The other two employees came marching into her office when they heard the news. "How could you do that to her?" they asked. "She's a single mom struggling to support two kids. Hire her back!" The optometrist explained the decision was not up for debate. The employees stood steadfast and responded, "If you don't hire her back, we both quit." It turned into a showdown. Put yourself in the optometrist's shoes. You began your day at 8:00 with three employees. By 8:30, you're down to two. You're facing the possibility of having no employees if you don't hire back the problem employee. What would your decision be?

There is no decision for the manager to make; it's already been made for her. She can't afford to hire back the problem employee. Her employees would be in control of her business if she did, and she would become powerless. Employees who give ultimatums like this are called terrorists—people who use force or threats to intimidate others. The United States has a firm policy on negotiating with terrorists: We *don't* negotiate. This must also be your policy. The optometrist stood her ground and showed her employees the door. They immediately backed down and said, "Oh, you didn't think we were serious, did you?" It worked like a charm, but she asked me a good question. She wanted to know what she should have done if the employees had walked out on her. The answer is to call a temporary service. She would be better off with three temporary employees who know nothing about the business but recognize her authority than with three veteran employees who know the business but with whom she is powerless. Managers hope it never comes to this, but it sometimes does. The owner of a window washing company who attended my "Managing Problem Employees" seminar in Waco, Texas, lost all six of his employees the same day. A hotel maintenance manager in Omaha, Nebraska, lost all eight of his employees his second week on the job. Both suffered in the short term.

Once they restaffed, both reaped the benefits of a new staff that respected their authority. Somebody has to be the captain of the ship. This is an irrefutable principle of management.

## I'm the Alpha Dog, You're Not!

The optometrist needed to define who the alpha dog was. If you're an avid dog lover like me, watch Animal Planet for a controversial maneuver called the alpha roll. Although you shouldn't try it at home because it's dangerous, it's amazing to watch. A professional dog trainer will use this maneuver when he needs to establish dominance with a defiant dog. He'll roll the dog over on its back and pin his paws down. He'll then put his face right in the dog's snout and scream, "I'm the alpha dog. You're not!" Watch what happens when the dog gets up. He'll hunch his rear end down to the ground like he's been physically beaten. This is metaphorically what the optometrist did with her employees. The manager of a women's clothing store in Burlington, Vermont, asked how she should respond if her employees really thought she was a heartless ogre for firing a single mother of two. My response to her was, "When did the manager become responsible for the employee's bad behavior?" The single mom shouldn't have risked losing her job if she needed it so badly. She received multiple warnings and ignored them all.

Another method aggressive subordinates will try is to challenge the validity of your authority with comments such as, "You're not my father!" Here's the speech to give in response to that comment:

> You're right. I'm not your father; I'm your boss. Just as your father was an authority figure in your life until you left home, I will be an authority figure in your life until you leave this company. You had the option to leave home anytime you decided you were no longer willing to respect your father's boundaries. You also have the option to leave here anytime you decide you are no longer willing to respect my boundaries. You are still here, so obviously you have chosen to respect them. You can expect me to be firm, fair, and consistent. I will expect you to be respectful, cooperative, and productive. As of this moment, I wish for you to remain a part of this team. Do you wish to remain a part of this team?

Why not respond with, "That's an inappropriate comment"? It would have been fine to respond this way, but it's better if you intentionally lose this small battle in order to win the war. While the comment was inappropriate, the employee gave you a gift. You have a perfect opportunity to turn the situation around and clarify the relationship. He isn't totally defiant; he would have walked out the door if he were. The fact that he is still there indicates he's acquiescing to your authority and is only testing a boundary. You have now clearly defined the dynamics of the relationship and reaffirmed the boundary. He will have to pay the piper if he violates it again in the future.

The key to managing aggressive people is to stand up to them. If you stand up to a bully, he'll become your best friend. Bullies are aggressive people. Aggressive people don't hang around other aggressive people; they hang around passive people they can push around. This is why weakness invites aggression.

## Understanding How Anger Works

While everyone gets angry, it is most often associated with being a hallmark of aggressive people. It is critical to understand how anger works in order to diffuse a situation. Angry people follow a very predictable pattern called the anger curve (Figure 7.1). Each point on the curve represents a different emotional stage. We all take this emotional roller coaster ride when we get angry. Think of it as an EKG of your emotions. The dotted line is the baseline of emotion.

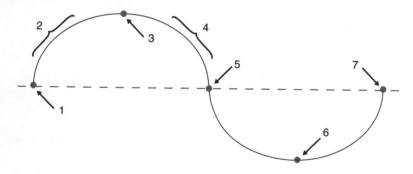

Figure 7.1   The Anger Curve

## Emotional Balance

People are in emotional balance at point 1. They're not in a vicious rage and they're not experiencing euphoric bliss. They're half way in between and their emotions are in check. This is most likely where you are as you read this book.

## Escalation

Emotions rise like mercury in a thermometer when people start to get angry. This is the escalation, which is phase 2. Not everyone's anger curve is as perfectly shaped and symmetrical as the one in Figure 7.1. You probably know people whose escalation looks more like a rocket that fires vertically. Regardless of how fast someone escalates, physical changes occur as they climb higher up the curve. Their shoulders draw back, breathing gets deeper, the heart accelerates, and their voice gets louder. Some people start to tremble, sweat, and flare their nostrils.

## The Point of Crisis

Point 3 is the first of two critical points you must be able to spot in employees as well as yourself. We can predict two characteristics when people hit this point. The first characteristic is poor judgment. People do things at point 3 they would never have done at point 1. The second characteristic is a diminished level of self-control. It's as if an alien force has taken over your body. Poor judgment and diminished self-control could also describe someone who is intoxicated, and this is how an angry person should be treated. You have to compensate for his poor judgment and diminished self-control with your good judgment and increased control of the situation. Because people don't think rationally at point 3, they always say things they later regret. This is why it is a bad idea to leave voice mail or send e-mail when you're angry.

## De-Escalation

People start to calm down after the temper tantrum has passed. This is the de-escalation, which is phase 4.

### Emotional Balance

Point 5 is the same as point 1. Physics tells us that we'll travel faster coming down a hill than we traveled when climbing it. This is what happens when we come down the anger curve. We can't put on our brakes and stop at the baseline of emotion where we started. The momentum causes us to shoot through point 5 and straight to point 6.

### The Anger Hangover

Point 6 is the second critical point on the anger curve. Imagine you had a big fight with your spouse just before leaving for work. You called him or her names, threatened divorce, gave ultimatums, and made all sorts of accusations. You slammed the door as you left, and could feel the adrenaline pumping like fire inside you. Later at work, you come down the anger curve hard. At point 6, you'll be overwhelmed with feelings of regret, remorse, and guilt. You'll worry this may be the straw that breaks the camel's back and your spouse may leave you this time. It's at this point that we all become very apologetic and make the promise we never keep. You'll call your spouse and swear that you'll never do it again. But you will do it again the next time you climb the anger curve. Just as you shouldn't say things at point 3 when you're in a rage of fury, you shouldn't make promises at point 6 when you're weak and vulnerable.

### Emotional Balance

When you return to emotional balance at point 7, you'll think clearly again.

## Forcing Angry People to De-Escalate

Now that you understand how anger works, you need to know why people get angry. Why does one person quietly work through unpleasant issues while another throws a temper tantrum? It isn't biological; it's learned behavior. People behave the way they behave because it works. People will change their behavior when it no longer gets the results they want.

Let's look at an example of changing behavior. A hotheaded employee comes into your office in the middle of a temper tantrum and tells you all about what just happened. Don't say, "I'm sorry this happened to you." This validates her anger, makes her a victim because something happened "to" her, and gives her sympathy. Instead, lead her toward a solution by helping her problem solve. Say something like "I understand you're angry, but there's nothing we can do about that now. What do we need to do to solve the problem?" Push the employee past the point of crisis and force her into de-escalation, and then into problem-solving mode. Note that even though you said "we," she will ultimately have to solve her own problem. Your role is only to guide her in that direction. Another response would be, "I've got to leave for a meeting in exactly four minutes. Tell me where you want us to be in this conversation in four minutes." When people are at point 3 on the anger curve, they will sometimes stay in their state of emotional constipation until somebody pushes them down the curve. Sometimes you have to be the emotional laxative for your employees.

The manager of a medical practice in Beaumont, Texas, had a unique solution for helping employees de-escalate without getting themselves into trouble. She encouraged employees to come to her when they were angry and needed to vent. She didn't want them taking out their temper tantrums on coworkers or patients, but also didn't want an employee to say something she would have to punish him for later. This sometimes created a dilemma. If the employee said the wrong thing and she had to punish him, he would never come to her again. If he didn't come to her, he might take out his anger in an inappropriate way. She devised a system she called the "anger envelope." She required the angry employee to write down what he was angry about. Next, she would insert it in an envelope that she placed in her in-basket. She would then tell the employee to come back 24 hours later and she would open the envelope. They would then discuss what was written. She also told the employee that if he changed his mind any time within the next 24 hours and decided he did not want her to read what he wrote, he could retrieve the envelope with no questions asked. In 20 years of using this method, not once did an employee fail to retrieve the envelope before 24 hours elapsed.

## The Passive-Aggressive Individual

Dealing with passive or aggressive people is relatively straightforward because both individuals are fairly consistent in their behavior. Passive-aggressive people are far more difficult because they're passive to your face, but attack when your back is turned. They don't fear all types of conflict like passives do; they only fear direct confrontation. Hence, they attack indirectly. This is why it's wise to keep your friends close and your enemies closer; you want to see the attack coming. This is easier said than done with passive-aggressive people. Their attacks can be so subtle that you never realize you're being attacked. They don't stick one big knife in your back; it's more like lots of little daggers. You'll feel as though you've been rubbing up against a porcupine all day long. It won't kill you, but all those little pricks get painful after a while. What makes it so difficult is that they can actually be quite charming to your face. Terms commonly associated with passive-aggressive people include:

- Breaking the chain of command
- Cheap shots
- Gossiping
- Pouting
- Revenge
- Sabotage
- Sarcasm
- Stabbing you in the back
- Spiteful
- Velvet-edged spikes

The key to managing passive-aggressive employees is to fight and win small battles at every opportunity, because major showdowns seldom occur. To win a battle with a passive-aggressive employee, always force a direct confrontation. You will win direct confrontations for two reasons: First, you're in the position of authority, so you have the upper hand. Second, direct confrontations put passive-aggressive people in a situation where they're least comfortable, and therefore least powerful. Let's look at an example.

One of the most common indicators of a passive-aggressive mentality is sarcasm; constantly taking cheap shots at everyone. To appreciate the seriousness of sarcasm, we have to look at the origin of the word. Sarcasm comes from the ancient Greek word sarkas-mos, which literally means, "to tear flesh." Military strategists know they can't win a war if they're out in the open and the enemy is hiding in the woods. Think of the sarcastic person as a sniper safely hidden in the woods while you're in the open and vulnerable. The best way to fight back is to draw the sniper out into the open.

Imagine that Susan takes a shot at you as soon as you walk into the office. She snarls, "Did somebody get up on the wrong side of the bed this morning?" She's really saying you're being a grouch, but a passive-aggressive person won't come right out and directly say what she really means. You must force it out of her. Respond with, "Exactly what did you mean by that comment?" She'll back down with "I didn't mean anything by it," and then try to slither away. This is the modus operandi for sarcastic people: hit and run. Call her back on the carpet with, "Obviously, you did mean something by it, or you wouldn't have said it to begin with. What did you mean by that personal attack on me?"

Because passive-aggressive people are so adept at finding ways to avoid direct conflict, she may try to slip out of the hotspot by turning the tables and making it about you. She resounds, "You just took it the wrong way." Come right back at her with "What's the right way to take a comment like that?" Maybe she goes even further and tries to make it a character flaw of yours by responding, "You're so hypersensitive. You need to loosen up." Again, don't let her off the hook. Come back at her with "I may or may not be, but it doesn't excuse your inappropriate comment. What did you mean by that personal attack on me?" By winning small battles like this, you'll start to see these subtle attacks slowly decrease over time.

## The Assertive Individual

The assertive model is the only healthy one, and the one that must best describe you if you are to succeed as a manager. Assertive managers clearly communicate to their employees what they hope for, what they expect, and what they won't tolerate. Your hopes for your employees are their goals, your expectations are their job duties, and your tolerance level is defined by boundaries.

Assertive managers hold everyone accountable. This includes their subordinates, their superiors, and themselves. An assertive manager is firm with her employees, while holding herself accountable for being fair and consistent. When her boss does something inappropriate, she holds her accountable as well. She is not insubordinate when she does, because she knows how to disagree but do so respectfully. She also knows when the boss overrides her, she has to comply. Assertive people also choose their battles wisely. They know every battle does not have to be fought or won.

## Conclusion

It is helpful for managers to understand the different behavioral types and why people do the things they do. It is imperative that managers understand human emotions in their employees, as well as themselves. Now that you have a basic understanding of why people behave the way they do, it's time to put that understanding into practice. In the next chapter, we look at how to win the battle against tardiness and absenteeism.

# CHAPTER 8

# How to Get Employees to Come to Work and Be on Time

I've never missed or arrived late at a speaking engagement in all the years I've been on the speaking circuit. The show must go on and I am the show. There certainly have been times when I had good excuses to not show up. I've been stranded in more airports than I can count. I've driven through blizzards, ice storms, tornadoes, and zero visibility fog to make it to the next hotel. Even after making it to the hotel, I'm not always safe. I've been in hotel fires in Pennsylvania, Rhode Island, Mississippi, and Tennessee. Once at a hotel in Chicago, the hotel maintenance engineer had to take the door to my room off the hinges after the electronic lock malfunctioned. Even when I make it to the seminar with no problems, there are days when I don't physically feel like speaking. I'll never forget the day in Haverhill, Massachusetts, when I had a 104 degree fever and could barely stand in the hotel room long enough to brush my teeth. Standing before a live audience for seven hours felt like a horrible punishment. I couldn't fly afterward and drove two days to get home. Then there was the time in Mobile, Alabama, when I lost my voice and had to whisper into a microphone all day. That day was even more memorable because I was scheduled to meet Tom Peters at lunch and didn't get to. I'll also never forget the time I spoke at Florida State University with the worst case of Montezuma's Revenge I've ever had. The attendees never figured out why we kept taking breaks every 30 minutes. There are also days when I feel fine physically but am unable to concentrate because of emotions. There was the seminar in Miami, Florida, after my father had a heart attack in Panama City. My mother assured me he was fine and there was no need to come immediately, but I was still torn by emotions. Then there was the seminar in Grand Rapids, Michigan, after the death of my beloved dog. I went back to my hotel room after the seminar that day and cried like a baby. I can remember every room I've ever spoken in and every audience except for those two. I was physically in Grand Rapids and Miami the days I had to be there, but my heart was elsewhere.

Even when I'm 100 percent and everything is going well beforehand, things happen during a live presentation that sometimes make me want to just throw the microphone down and go home. I'll never forget doing a seven-hour seminar soaked in sweat in Abilene, Texas. It was July 2003 and the temperature in West Texas was well over 100 degrees. The air conditioner wasn't working and the ballroom felt like a sauna. I was glad I was wearing a cordless microphone because I was sure I would have been electrocuted if I were wired. Then there was the time in Ann Arbor, Michigan, when I used a cordless microphone for the first time and forgot to turn it off when I went to the restroom. I did not want to finish that seminar, but kept focused by remembering a show I saw Jay Leno give at a casino in Tunica, Mississippi. His microphone went dead in the middle of his big opening. He already had a long-term contract to host *The Tonight Show*, and didn't need to do stand-up comedy in a casino in the middle of nowhere. He did it to practice new material and stay on top of his game. He worked the dead microphone into his monologue and continued as if it had been planned. I copied Leno and joked with my audience that somebody was piping mysterious sound effects into the PA system. I'll never know if they bought it, but I finished that day slightly more seasoned than when I began.

## Professionalism and Absenteeism

I make sure that I am on time and am fully prepared for every seminar or speech. I always do the job I am paid to do for the same reason as Leno: *professionalism*. Professionalism means doing your best even when you don't feel like it. A manager in Kansas asked me how to get his employees who are not quite as dedicated to their jobs to demonstrate the same level of professionalism. My answer was, "That's not possible." Employees who are not dedicated to their jobs will not be that dependable. However, any organization can establish a culture and image of dependability. The U.S. Post Office is a great example. Despite all the haranguing it receives for employees "going postal," it also has a reputation for reliability. We all expect the mail carrier to deliver the mail through rain, sleet, snow, or hail. Competitors such as FedEx, DHL, and UPS know they have to play the game at the highest level of professionalism to compete. No one ever questions whether a package will arrive on time based on who called in sick on a given day. We expect all four carriers to deliver on time regardless of their staffing situations. It is up to you to define the standard for your company. Do you want to be as professional and reliable as FedEx? If so, you'll have to define clear boundaries of what you will tolerate regarding absenteeism and tardiness.

## What Is reasonable?

The next question that must be answered is what is reasonable as far as tardiness and absenteeism. The answer depends on the business. In manufacturing, an employee who is one minute late can create a financial disaster called *bottlenecking*. When 300 employees are on a production line, each must be present in order for the others to do their jobs. The comptroller for an automobile manufacturing plant told me they lose approximately $10,000 per minute for every minute production is delayed.

Absenteeism and tardiness can be even more expensive for small companies. Day care centers are required to keep certain ratios of employees to children. If too many employees are running late or out sick on the day state inspectors pay a visit, then the state can put the center out of business. Some school districts are taking the problem of absenteeism with students to the highest level. Evansville, Indiana, authorities charge parents with a criminal misdemeanor if their child has more than 15 unexcused absences. You must decide how important punctuality and attendance are in your organization. Once you decide what is reasonable, then the task becomes a matter of enforcing the limits.

## What Doesn't Work

I once attended a seminar in Detroit, Michigan, where the speaker suggested the way to handle an 8:00 A.M. to 5:00 P.M. employee who constantly drags in at 8:07 is to change his schedule to 9:00 A.M. to 6:00 P.M. It is obvious this man has never supervised anyone. Any experienced manager knows this employee will then drag in at 9:07 A.M. The problem isn't the hours: It's the behavior. The same speaker suggested an equally inept solution to absenteeism. He recommended companies pay a bonus of $100 for every 90 days an employee has perfect attendance. Again he demonstrated that he never managed anyone. Managers who have tried this know the employees who always earn the bonus are the ones who would have come to work on time anyway. The ones who never earn the bonus are the ones whose behavior the bonus was meant to change. A $100 bonus is not enough incentive to get people to change. If an employee makes $8 an hour, he will gross about $4,000 every 90 days. An additional $100 amounts to about a 2 percent bonus, which is not enough to get an unmotivated employee to improve his attendance. If it were, then giving a 2 percent raise would solve the problem.

Bonuses only work if they're substantial enough to have a drastic or immediate impact. Continental Airlines gathers the names of all employees with perfect attendance every six months. Names randomly selected from this group receive a new Ford Explorer. This not only improves attendance, but also boosts moral. This obviously won't be realistic for most companies. Managers must find the best methods to reward the good behavior and punish the bad in order to prevent excessive absenteeism and tardiness.

## Rewarding Punctuality

The best reward I've seen for getting hourly employees to come to work on time is hourly incentive pay. It is extremely radical but works wonders when administered properly. One reason bonuses normally don't solve the problem of tardiness is because they don't provide immediate gratification. As we discussed in Chapter 7, the consequences of bad behavior must outweigh the pleasure of being bad in order to motivate people to be good. The immediate gratification of hitting the snooze bar when the alarm clock goes off and staying in bed a little longer is enticing. If the only punishment is losing a bonus that won't be paid for another three months, the reward is too distant for most people. This is similar to trying to withstand the present temptation of the Bloomin' Onion in order to be slender at some distant point in the future.

Hourly incentive pay gives employees immediate gratification they can sink their teeth into every Friday. Imagine an employee is hired at $8 an hour. No matter what she does, she's guaranteed $8 an hour. If she comes to work on time Monday morning, she earns a $1 per hour bonus for the rest of the week. This makes her effective rate $9 per hour for the week. She earns an additional $1 per hour bonus by clocking in on time again Tuesday, Wednesday, Thursday, and Friday. Each additional $1 per hour is retroactive to Monday morning at eight o'clock. By getting to work on time each day of the week, she effectively ends up with a rate of $13 per hour for the week. This amounts to a $200 bonus. So why not just pay a $200 bonus for the week? Adding the bonus as a lump sum doesn't work as well as the hourly rate, even though the math comes out the same. This isn't about math; this is about human behavior and immediate gratification. Progressive companies utilizing this method understand the benefit of breaking bonuses down to an hourly basis. This method of breaking larger numbers down comes from advertising and sales. An insurance agent knows he will sell more insurance by quoting it as, "less than $2 a day" than by quoting it as, "$59 a month."

Paying an extra $200 per week for perfect attendance seems steep until a secret is known. The company using this method intended to pay the employee $13 an hour from the beginning. The compensation was restructured so that the $13 hourly rate is no longer an entitlement; it's an incentive. Some employers have tried starting the employee at the higher rate and then deducting the $1 per hour for each day the employee is late. This should not be done because it creates some legal ambiguity. An employer who promises $13 an hour and ends up paying $6 an hour may receive a visit from the Department of Labor. There are no laws against paying as much of a bonus as an employer chooses to pay. The $1 per hour figure will be unrealistic for many companies. Managers who have attended my seminars have reported success with hourly incentive pay as low as 25 cents per hour. Higher amounts are best, but the concept can work at any level.

## Rewarding Good Attendance

The manager of a small-town water department attended my seminar at Arkansas State University. His city charter granted employees five paid sick days per year. There was no provision for buying back unused sick days, and employees could not carry them forward to the next year. The city had a "use 'em or lose 'em" policy. Starting around December 26, everyone started "using 'em." He asked me how to solve this employee problem. He didn't have an employee problem; he had a policy problem. An employee with perfect attendance as of December 26 will be working for free the last week of the year. He would make the same amount of money by staying at home and watching the college football games all week. There must be a reward for not using sick days. At a bare minimum, companies should allow employees to accrue unused sick days.

A more effective approach is to buy them back. Imagine that an employee is allowed five paid sick days and normally earns $100 a day. At the end of the year, he can sell his unused days back to the company for $100 a day. This makes the year-end bonus $500 with perfect attendance. Other organizations with tighter budgets may discount the rate and buy back the time at $50 per day. This isn't as rewarding as full dollar-for-dollar buyback, but it's better than nothing. Using this rate, the employee with $500 of unused sick time would receive $250 when selling it back. Companies that place a higher premium on perfect attendance will go in the opposite direction. They'll pay double time to buy back unused sick days from employees with perfect attendance. Their philosophy is that employees will make twice as much for being healthy as they would make for being sick. Using this rate, the employee with $500 of unused sick time would be able to sell it back for $1,000. Some companies take it further by adjusting the buy-back rate based on attendance. The better the employee's attendance, the higher his or her buy-back rate. Here is an example for an employee who normally makes $100 a day:

| Unused Sick Days | Buy-Back Rate | Effective Amount per Day |
|---|---|---|
| 5 | $2.00 per $1 | $200 |
| 4 | $1.75 per $1 | $175 |
| 3 | $1.50 per $1 | $150 |
| 2 | $1.25 per $1 | $125 |
| 1 | $1 per $1 | $100 |

## Punishing Excessive Absenteeism and Attendance

Now that we have discussed rewards for good behavior, we must consider the punishment for bad behavior. One of the most radical methods for punishing employees who come to work a few minutes late is called "Detention Hall." An employee who comes in 5 minutes late Monday morning has to stay 5 minutes late to make up the time. He doesn't make it up Monday. Instead, the accumulated 5 minutes from Monday morning, 3 minutes from Tuesday morning, 2 minutes from Wednesday morning, 10 minutes from Thursday morning, and 10 minutes from Friday morning are made up Friday afternoon. Staying a few minutes late Monday through Thursday won't faze most people, but staying 30 minutes late Friday afternoon hurts. An even more radical spin on detention hall is the team approach. Not only is the tardy employee required to make up time on Friday, but so is everyone else. The peer pressure becomes so severe that the employee either gets his act together or is run off by his coworkers. This method is not advisable for most organizations and wouldn't be legal to use on hourly employees unless the others were paid overtime. However, it does produce amazing results. It is sometimes used on salaried employees who work closely as a self-directed team. When we discuss this radical method in seminars, managers sometimes ask, "But isn't this degrading to the employee?" My answer is, "Absolutely." The next question is, "Why would you want to degrade an employee?" My response to this question is the same as it was to the question regarding the single mother who lost her job in Chapter 7, "When did the manager become responsible for the employee's bad behavior?" The purpose of using this radical method is to prevent the bad behavior. The employee who chooses to constantly break the rules is degrading himself. If he doesn't want to be punished, he shouldn't break the rules.

The fairest, oldest, and most practical method is a point system. Points are assigned to employees as schools assign demerits to students. Some companies call them occurrences. A basic system works like this:

One tardy = ½ point

One absence = 1 point

One absence without calling in = 2 points

At 6 points, the employee is terminated. One year after the date of the occurrence, the point or fraction of a point assigned for that occurrence drops off his record. Under this system, the employee can't accumulate more than 6 points within any 12-month period. The

6-point cap is only an example, and can be adjusted up or down based on what you think is reasonable. The number is not important; the concept is. You are setting a clear limit on how much tardiness and absenteeism you will tolerate.

A more sophisticated system prorates the points by how tardy the employee is:

Up to 15 minutes late = ¼ of a point

16 to 30 minutes late = ½ of a point

31 to 45 minutes late = ¾ of a point

46 minutes up to 1 hour late = 1 full point

One full day absent (8 hours) = 8 points

If you require that employees give you advance notice when calling out sick, you can also work this into the system. If you require a one-hour advance notice, an employee who calls out sick but gives you one-hour notice might receive 8 points. If he gives less than an hour notice, he receives 10 points. If he calls in after his scheduled start time, he receives 12 points. If he doesn't call in at all, he receives 16 points. It is also common for companies to assign double the normal points for missing critical days such as those before or after holidays. The roll-off mechanism for this is monthly. For each 30 days of perfect attendance, 8 points are subtracted. At 50 points (or whatever cutoff level you choose), the employee is terminated. There must be two exceptions to this system. First, the Family Medical Leave Act requires covered companies to give up to 12 weeks unpaid leave time for certain mostly medical-related issues. Second, there needs to be a provision for a catastrophic illness or injury. This system isn't intended to punish an employee who is in a coma for three months. This system punishes the employee who has a different excuse every week.

## Conclusion

In doing research for my next book, *How to Be Indispensable: 21 Ways to Become Priceless to Your Employer,* I conducted an online survey of nearly 7,000 managers and asked them what they most desired in an employee.[1] The most common answer was "to show up for work, and be on time." This sounds like so little to ask. Yet, it remains another difficult battle to win. Winning this one truly makes you a professional manager. In the next chapter, we look at how to properly discipline employees, without necessarily punishing them.

# CHAPTER 9

# The Art of Discipline

Termination is the one task managers hope to never get too much practice at doing. It requires starting the process of interviewing, hiring, and training all over again. There are also unemployment benefits, the threat of litigation, and the possibility of physical violence or other retaliation. Making the process even more unsavory is the barrage of emotions associated with it. There's the nagging doubt of whether the employee received enough chances before he was fired. This doubt can turn into guilt and plague managers incessantly. The decision to keep a struggling employee carries with it the uncertainty of how long is too long. Properly handling discipline can eliminate these emotions. It ultimately becomes the employee's choice to lose his job. Turning a bad employee into a good employee is a realistic goal; expecting to achieve this with everyone is not. There is no definitive standard for deciding when to fire an employee. There is, however, an art to discipline.

## How Many Chances Should an Employee Get?

We all know people who have given kids, spouses, and friends so many chances to stop screwing up that it eventually became a joke.

Bill Clinton swore to Hillary that Gennifer Flowers was his last tryst. During the 1992 presidential campaign, Hillary told reporters that she and her husband had dealt with the matter privately. She stated she would leave him if he did it again. Regardless of whether I agree or disagree with her politics, I felt empathy for her as a human being after the Monica Lewinsky scandal broke. Only she could decide how many more chances to give him; it was her decision and hers alone. For whatever reason, she decided to stay. It clearly yielded positive results for her. She went from First Lady to U.S. senator.

Managers ask me how many chances an employee should get. The answer does not lie in a number but in your judgment. Continue giving the employee chances as long as you believe three facts to be true:

1. He is capable of succeeding.
2. He is giving 100 percent in his effort to succeed.
3. Your investment will pay off within a reasonable amount of time.

The employee decides if the first two conditions will be met. Nothing else matters if he is not capable of doing the job. Good intentions and all the motivation in the world are insufficient when an employee is in over his head. If he is capable of doing the job, he must be willing to exert enough effort to achieve the results you desire.

Assuming the first two conditions are met, you will have to make a decision on the third. Most people will eventually come around. You would know better than to hire those who are incorrigible. The question regarding most problem employees is not whether they will get with the program, but *when* they will get with the program. We can't afford to invest the time it would take to salvage some people.

## Calculate Your Return on Investment

Hiring a new employee is an investment in the future. You're gambling that your investment will pay dividends at some point. Financial experts recommend against investing in the stock market unless you plan to leave the money alone for at least five years. We don't have that kind of time to wait for a return on investment (ROI) from employees. While we hope all employees will be long-term investments, we know most will not. Since the average job lasts about three years, this should be your long-term horizon in evaluating the ROI for an employee. Hope that you will keep him longer, but be prepared for less. We must also get a short-term ROI in employees. Because everyone climbs the learning curve at a different pace, the short-term ROI will be different for every employee. The long-term ROI in an employee has to be the highest of any investment you will ever make. It must be 100 percent or more. If it is less than 100 percent, the employee is costing more than he's worth. Every employee must eventually earn his paycheck. This is more easily quantified for some jobs than others. A surgeon who hits the ground running with multiple surgeries every day earns her paycheck immediately. A rookie quarterback who leads his team to the Superbowl his first season earns his paycheck immediately. A salesperson who exceeds her quota the first week earns her paycheck immediately.

Most people don't earn their paychecks immediately, myself included. I self-published for 10 years. If I sold enough books, I made money. If I sold nothing, I didn't make a dime. That changed when I signed with the publisher of this book. I received my first advance nine months before the release date. The publisher invested in me knowing they would not receive an ROI for nearly a year. They took four huge gambles. They gambled that:

1. I was capable of writing a 60,000 word manuscript.
2. I would actually sit down and get it done.
3. I would get it finished in the allotted time.
4. It would sell well enough to bring a sufficient ROI.

They made an investment with a time frame to limit their losses, knowing the odds were overwhelmingly against both of us. But just in case I do become the rookie quarterback who leads his team to the Superbowl his first year, they made sure to keep me on their team by optioning my next book. All they expect is for me to be a player who earns my keep. They will invest time, money, and effort into publishing me as long as they believe the investment will pay off. The same should be true with your employees. Work backward from the three-year horizon and ask yourself how much time, money, and effort you are willing to invest.

Also take into account the opportunity cost. For every dollar you invest in mutual funds, single stocks, or certificates of deposit, you have one dollar less to purchase a home or send your kids to college. We all have a limited number of dollars to invest. Likewise, managers have limited resources. Every minute and ounce of energy we invest in an employee is one we cannot invest in others. Every dollar we spend on attempting to salvage an employee is a dollar we can't use to buy a new piece of equipment, hire another employee, or use to reward an existing employee. At some point, we have to cut our losses. Before reaching the decision to do this, we want to make sure we have exhausted every possibility of correcting bad behavior. This is where the art of discipline can be a lifesaver.

## Progressive Discipline

The three golden rules of management are document, document, document. If you stay in management, the day will come when you will be kicking yourself for not having documented enough. Creating the perfect paper trail can provide tremendous legal benefits. It can help win claims for unemployment benefits, prove that the employee knew his job was in jeopardy, and prove you were fair and consistent. Most importantly, it can salvage employees who are teetering on the edge.

Remember that as an employer-at-will you have the legal right to terminate an employee at any time without prior notice. Progressive discipline is used when a manager believes an employee's bad behavior is not severe enough to warrant immediate termination. It does not mean that an employee is guaranteed multiple chances to change. Labor lawyers often advise management not to mention the progressive discipline process in employee manuals so that it cannot be used to argue that an implied contract exists. At the same time, progressive discipline provides the best paper trail possible. An example of progressive discipline is outlined next.

## Step One: Verbal Warning

The employee receives a verbal warning the first time bad behavior occurs. Explain:

- What he did wrong.
- How the behavior should be corrected.
- That his job is in jeopardy if the behavior continues.
- That you don't want to lose him, but his future is up to him.

The verbal warning should be thoroughly documented. Document where the conversation occurred, when it occurred, and the name of any supervisor who witnessed it. Then have the witnessing supervisor sign it. Do not have the employee sign it; his signature could make it look like a written warning, which would defeat the purpose of progressive discipline. The employee could then sue for wrongful termination by arguing that he never received a verbal warning and didn't understand his job was in jeopardy. This documentation is for your benefit, not his.

## Step Two: Written Warning

The employee receives a written warning the second time the behavior occurs. Begin with a recap of the verbal warning, and then go through the entire process again. When finished, have him sign the written warning. When he signs the written warning, which references the verbal warning, he acknowledges he received the verbal warning as well as the written. This acknowledgment proves he knew his job was in jeopardy. Give him space to write a rebuttal. Even if he disagrees, it is advantageous to get the written rebuttal because it proves he received the warning. If he refuses to sign it, mail a copy to his house by certified mail. His signature on the postal receipt will now become your proof that he received the warning. If he refuses to sign for certified mail, send it by UPS with signature required for delivery.

### Step Three: Decision-Making Leave

The employee is suspended the third time the behavior occurs. As we discussed in Chapter 7, a three-day unpaid suspension could actually be a vacation. To prevent this, employers use a decision-making leave. The employee is still suspended, but it's a paid suspension with strings attached. The manager informs the employee that he is close to losing his job. What happens next is up to him. He is to spend the next three days deciding what he wants his future with the company to be. If he decides he wants to keep his job, he must formulate a personal improvement plan to get himself back on track. This should be in writing, and you should specify how long it has to be. A reasonable length would be 2,000 words. One manager in Augusta, Georgia, had a slight variation. Instead of writing a personal improvement plan, he required his employees to read *Who Moved My Cheese* and write a book report on it.[1]

The manager of a hair salon in Saginaw, Michigan, told me she has used decision-making leaves five times. Four employees came back with an attitude adjustment. The fifth called in during her decision-making leave to announce she found a different job. The outcomes were different, but the problem was solved with all five employees. Other companies call the personal improvement plan a commitment to improve. The term is not important, but the concept is. The concept is that these companies are doing everything in their power to salvage employees who are salvageable. They're also creating the best paper trail possible to protect themselves in case the employee is later terminated. If it gets to that point, it will be clear the employee chose to leave his job.

### Step Four: Probation

In one last-ditch effort to cover all bases, employers will sometimes give an employee a final 90- to 180-day probationary period. The employer explains to the employee that he has essentially lost his job. However, the employer wants to exhaust all remedies and is giving the employee one last chance to prove why he is worthy of keeping his job. If he can be a model employee during this probationary period, the process will start back at the beginning. If he can't, the game's over.

## Step Five: Termination

Management is not a science. It is an art, and it is a very delicate art. Deciding when to cut your losses and move on is one of the most difficult decisions a manager can face. When you come to the point of deciding the employee is a lost cause, don't continue pouring good money after bad and hoping the employee will miraculously have an epiphany. You'll only end up delaying the inevitable. When it's time for the employee to go, it's time for the employee to go. The sooner you cut your losses and move forward, the sooner you can start plowing your valuable resources into a better investment.

## Breaking Up Is Hard to Do

The system is so biased against employers that it has almost forgotten managers are employees, too. The aftermath of firing an employee can be just as serious for the boss as for the employee. A certain sense of failure and disappointment looms in the air during the first moment after the employee leaves. There's that nagging self-doubt of whether it was the right thing to do. Was I too harsh? Did I let it go on too long?

Many experts on stress list losing a job as one of the most stressful events in life. It is consistently ranked high along with the death of a family member, divorce, and filing for bankruptcy. I have not heard any of these experts address the stress a manager feels after firing an employee. Police officers are required to talk to a counselor after shooting a suspect. Doctors hold morbidity and mortality conferences after losing patients. They discuss what went wrong and what they can learn from it. Losing a patient is an agonizing event for a physician; it is also inevitable. The same is true for managers who terminate employees. Talk to upper management when it happens. It's natural to feel a little guilty after firing someone. It's also unnecessary. You tried to salvage the employee by giving him every chance to save his job. He fired himself, and you can go to sleep with a clear conscious. This battle is over and there's no benefit to dwelling on it. You'll live to fight another day.

## Spontaneous Termination

Certain behavior should warrant immediate termination. Even if the behavior is not that outrageous, employment-at-will allows you to fire an employee just because you are tired of dealing with him. Some managers ask, "But is this fair to the employee?" My response is, "Why do businesses exist?" Businesses exist to make a profit; they do not exist to provide jobs. Not even nonprofit organizations exist to provide jobs; they exist to provide a service to their clients. If an employee is detracting from an organization's ability to achieve its goal, the employee needs to go. Even those who insist businesses have a social obligation to provide jobs can't justify keeping problem employees. If an employee is not beneficial to the business, he jeopardizes the jobs of other employees. When people insist on placing employees' interests before the company's interests, my question is, "Which employee's interests come first, the good employee's, or the problem employee's?" No organization should punish its good employees by keeping bad employees. Managers have to make decisions that are best for the organization they are managing, and some of those decisions need to be made rather quickly. If an employee insists on being dangerous, disruptive, destructive, or counterproductive, get rid of him as soon as possible. A supervisor from a dynamite factory said, "I'm not going to give an employee five warnings not to smoke beside the dynamite!"

## Conclusion

Retired General Electric CEO and management guru Jack Welch says that firing people is the most unpleasant part of any manager's job. He also says that it is inevitable. Managers cannot control whether an employee chooses to get fired. Managers can only control whether employees who wish to keep their jobs have sufficient opportunity to do so. In the next chapter, we look at one of the battles that isn't a major war, but is a major nuisance that can crop up after terminating an employee—abuse of unemployment benefits.

CHAPTER

# Fighting Abuse of Unemployment Benefits

Nothing angers business owners more than paying unemployment benefits. It is the most sensitive hot button I've ever come across in my years of studying, teaching, and practicing management. It is also the most confusing. To fight abuse of unemployment benefits, managers first need to understand how the system works. Most employers are required to pay state unemployment insurance tax (SUTA) and federal unemployment insurance tax (FUTA). Nonprofit organizations don't pay until a terminated employee wins a claim. In theory, an employee is entitled to receive weekly payments for up to 26 weeks when he loses his job through no fault of his own. The effective rate for FUTA is 0.8 percent for most employers. It is assessed on only the first $7,000 each employee earns each year, meaning most employers pay $56 per employee per year. This remains constant no matter how much the employee earns or how many employees draw unemployment benefits. This is tolerable.

What makes business owners so angry is the state unemployment tax. States calculate the SUTA rate using ratios of what a company has paid into the fund versus the current payroll. This percentage increases when terminated employees draw unemployment benefits or when payroll increases. Each state also sets its own wage base. Eleven states match the federal wage base of $7,000, while the others are all higher. The highest is Hawaii's, which is currently $32,300. This makes their state wage base more than four times the federal wage base. Seventeen states also increased their wage base in 2005. Table 10.1 lists the 2002–2005 wage bases.

All managers should know what their company's SUTA rate is. If you don't, find out immediately. The percentage will appear on the form your company files with your state department of employment security. If your rate is above zero, ask them to examine your account and determine when your rate will be lowered. Do not delegate this task to your CPA. You need to know your SUTA rate and monitor the changes, even if your CPA files the actual report. One seminar attendee called during the lunch break and got his rate lowered to zero. If you own the company, you will be putting money in your pocket by getting this rate lowered. It won't be a huge amount, but it will be enough to pay for this book. If you don't own the company, this is an easy way to earn some serious points with the owner.

## Why Unemployment Benefits Are a Sham

Unemployment compensation was created in the 1930s as part of President Franklin D. Roosevelt's New Deal, which also created welfare and Social Security, as discussed in Chapter 1. Our country was trying to recover from the Great Depression, and the concept was idealistic at the time. The system is mostly a sham today, doesn't achieve its stated goals, and is more abused than welfare. People will not be driven to find work as long as the government pays them enough to get by. The definition of compensation is to make up for or counterbalance something. The fact that it is called unemployment benefits instead of unemployment compensation tells the

## Table 10.1
### 2005 Wage Bases for Unemployment Insurance

| State | 2005 ($) | 2004 ($) | 2003 ($) | 2002 ($) |
|---|---|---|---|---|
| Alabama | $ 8,000 | $ 8,000 | $ 8,000 | $ 8,000 |
| Alaska | 27,900 | 27,100 | 26,700 | 26,000 |
| Arizona | 7,000 | 7,000 | 7,000 | 7,000 |
| Arkansas | 10,000 | 10,000 | 9,500 | 9,000 |
| California | 7,000 | 7,000 | 7,000 | 7,000 |
| Colorado | 10,000 | 10,000 | 10,000 | 10,000 |
| Connecticut | 15,000 | 15,000 | 15,000 | 15,000 |
| Delaware | 8,500 | 8,500 | 8,500 | 8,500 |
| D.C. | 9,000 | 9,000 | 9,000 | 9,000 |
| Florida | 7,000 | 7,000 | 7,000 | 7,000 |
| Georgia | 8,500 | 8,500 | 8,500 | 8,500 |
| Hawaii | 32,300 | 31,000 | 30,200 | 29,300 |
| Idaho | 28,000 | 27,600 | 27,600 | 27,600 |
| Illinois | 10,500 | 9,800 | 9,000 | 9,000 |
| Indiana | 7,000 | 7,000 | 7,000 | 7,000 |
| Iowa | 20,400 | 19,700 | 19,200 | 18,600 |
| Kansas | 8,000 | 8,000 | 8,000 | 8,000 |
| Kentucky | 8,000 | 8,000 | 8,000 | 8,000 |
| Louisiana | 7,000 | 7,000 | 7,000 | 7,000 |
| Maine | 12,000 | 12,000 | 12,000 | 12,000 |
| Maryland | 8,500 | 8,500 | 8,500 | 8,500 |
| Massachusetts | 14,000 | 14,000 | 10,800 | 10,800 |
| Michigan | 9,000 | 9,000 | 9,500 | 9,500 |
| Minnesota | 23,000 | 22,000 | 22,000 | 21,000 |
| Mississippi | 7,000 | 7,000 | 7,000 | 7,000 |
| Missouri | 11,000 | 8,000 | 7,500 | 7,000 |
| Montana | 21,000 | 20,300 | 19,700 | 18,900 |
| Nebraska | 7,000 | 7,000 | 7,000 | 7,000 |
| Nevada | 22,900 | 22,000 | 21,500 | 20,900 |
| New Hampshire | 8,000 | 8,000 | 8,000 | 8,000 |
| New Jersey | 24,900 | 24,300 | 23,900 | 23,500 |
| New Mexico | 17,200 | 16,800 | 16,600 | 15,900 |
| New York | 8,500 | 8,500 | 8,500 | 8,500 |
| North Carolina | 16,700 | 16,200 | 15,900 | 15,500 |
| North Dakota | 19,400 | 18,500 | 18,000 | 17,400 |

(*continued*)

Table 10.1 (Continued)

| State | 2005 ($) | 2004 ($) | 2003 ($) | 2002 ($) |
|---|---|---|---|---|
| Ohio | 9,000 | 9,000 | 9,000 | 9,000 |
| Oklahoma | 13,800 | 14,300 | 11,700 | 10,500 |
| Oregon | 27,000 | 27,000 | 26,000 | 25,000 |
| Pennsylvania | 8,000 | 8,000 | 8,000 | 8,000 |
| Puerto Rico | 7,000 | 7,000 | 7,000 | 7,000 |
| Rhode Island | 16,000 | 14,000 | 12,000 | 12,000 |
| South Carolina | 7,000 | 7,000 | 7,000 | 7,000 |
| South Dakota | 7,000 | 7,000 | 7,000 | 7,000 |
| Tennessee | 7,000 | 7,000 | 7,000 | 7,000 |
| Texas | 9,000 | 9,000 | 9,000 | 9,000 |
| Utah | 23,200 | 22,700 | 22,500 | 22,000 |
| Vermont | 8,000 | 8,000 | 8,000 | 8,000 |
| Virgin Islands | 18,600 | 18,400 | 18,000 | 16,800 |
| Virginia | 8,000 | 8,000 | 8,000 | 8,000 |
| Washington | 30,500 | 30,200 | 29,700 | 28,500 |
| West Virginia | 8,000 | 8,000 | 8,000 | 8,000 |
| Wisconsin | 10,500 | 10,500 | 10,500 | 10,500 |
| Wyoming | 16,400 | 15,900 | 14,700 | 14,700 |

story. A benefit contributes to the improvement of something or somebody. Paying fraudulent claims for unemployment benefits hardly contributes to anyone's well being. The first problem with unemployment benefits is that there is no means test to determine if the individual actually needs the money. Benefits are handed out indiscriminately, and often go to secondary wage earners who are enduring no financial hardship.

The second problem is the certification process. States require the recipient to actively seek work while receiving the benefits. The assumption is that recipients really want to work but can't find a job. This might have been true during the Great Depression, but is rarely true today. Most people do not actively seek work and states don't verify their so-called attempts. A colleague told me that when she worked in a shoe store as a teenager in the 1980s, people would regularly come in at night to inquire if they were hiring. Applications weren't taken at night, so she would tell them to come back during the day when the manager was present. Most never did. When she told them they did not take applications at night, they'd ask her to sign a form indicating they sought employment with the store. These individuals were not looking for companies that were hiring; they were looking for fully staffed companies to show they were actively seeking work in order to continue receiving unemployment benefit checks. It is even easier to maintain certification today. Recipients in most states simply call and answer questions asked by a computer. The computer asks, "Are you actively looking for employment? Press 1 for yes and 2 for no." All a recipient has to do to continue receiving a weekly check is press a button; no proof is required. Millions of dollars are given away based on the honor system. In my hometown, we require more from homeless people to get a free meal than the state requires from unemployed people to get a free check. I interviewed the director of the Nashville Rescue Mission, who informed me they do not turn away people in need. However, they require clients to exert some effort to utilize their services. Transients must attend chapel service each night in order to stay in the shelter. Those in long-term recovery must attend classes, meet with counselors, and work at the shelter in order to stay for up to seven months. As they progress, they get to move into nicer accommodations. Rick Warren, author of *The Purpose Driven Life,* requires every person who joins his church to contribute something. An attorney may volunteer her services to help with estate planning for members. A mechanic might volunteer his services to fix a car for a struggling family. This homeless shelter in Tennessee and mega church in California rightfully require those who seek their help to do something in exchange for it, while the government continues mailing unemployment checks to people who can maintain eligibility without getting out of bed.

The third problem with unemployment benefits is in the math. Assume I fire an employee for no fault of his own. Under Tennessee law, the individual can receive up to $275 a week for up to 26 weeks. This equates to almost $6.88 per hour for a 40-hour a week job. If this same individual took a minimum wage job at $5.15 an hour, he would receive nearly $70 per week less. He now has a decision to make. He can get out of bed and go to work for the next 26 weeks to make $5,356, or he could do nothing and make $7,176. This discourages people from working. I looked up current federal policy on unemployment benefits in the House Ways and Means Committee 2004 Green Book, and found it was even worse than I previously thought. Not only does the government discourage the employee from working at the $5.15 per hour job, but it also protects him from having to do so. The law states the employee is not required to take a job that pays less than what he draws in unemployment benefits. Even if the money were equal, an individual working at a temporary job he doesn't like will find a more desirable job much faster than if he was doing nothing. The government is rewarding laziness.

The fourth problem is that employers are punished today for a "crime" they may or may not commit in the future. In the chilling sci-fi movie *Minority Report,* we saw political correctness at its worst. Tom Cruise played a cop who arrested people for crimes before the crimes were committed. It sounded far-fetched, but something similar happens with unemployment insurance. States try to predict how likely a company is to fire or lay off employees before it happens. The state then taxes the employer according to the predictions. Most new businesses are assigned a 2.7 percent SUTA rate. This means that new businesses in a state with a $7,000 wage base will pay $189 per employee per year. As time goes by and more payments are made, this rate would fall assuming payroll remains consistent and no one draws unemployment benefits. I met a general contractor in Des Moines, Iowa, who was assigned a 10 percent SUTA rate because he was in construction. Iowa now has a wage base of $20,400, which costs him $2,040 per employee per year. He has 52 employees, which means he is paying over $106,000 a year. Some naive souls claim they wouldn't mind paying this much if they owned a company that large. Yes, they would! Nobody wants to pay for something they haven't done and may never do. Imagine how you would feel if the IRS required you to prepay income taxes on money before you earned it, based on how much they thought you might earn. Even for the self-employed who file quarterly estimates of personal income tax, the estimates are calculated on the previous year's actual income. The IRS is fairer than the state departments of employment security.

The fifth problem is that good employees are punished because of bad employees. At a bare minimum, unemployment insurance should be handled for all companies as it is handled for nonprofits. The state should not charge a company until a claim is filed. I have paid SUTA taxes for 17 years, but never had anyone draw against me. I could have used the thousands of dollars the state has taken from my company to pay year-end bonuses to my hard-working employees. Instead, my employees indirectly suffer in order to protect bad employees who I may never hire and may never fire. I can never get the money back, but am forced to continue paying.

The sixth problem is that people still draw benefits even when it was their fault that they lost their job. The newest nemesis for employers is called "suicide by supervisor," where an employee takes a job with a company in order to get himself fired. Being fired is not his punishment; it's his goal. He stays with the company just long enough to qualify for unemployment benefits and then does something blatantly wrong that will result in termination. Next, he convinces some government bureaucrat that he was an innocent victim who didn't understand his job was in jeopardy. They in turn reward him with a weekly check.

The seventh problem with unemployment benefits is that they can be charged against the previous employer who had nothing to do with the employee losing his job. This is the ultimate slap in the face for the employer.

## How to Win Claims for Unemployment Benefits

As with claims of racial discrimination or sexual harassment, employers are presumed guilty until proven innocent when claims for unemployment benefits are filed. This is another difficult battle to win. Many state departments of employment security are so biased against employers, it almost borders on hostility. The web page for one state department of employment security reads:

If an individual is discharged by his or her employer and the employer documents misconduct connected to the work, the separation would be disqualified. If an individual voluntarily quits his or her employment for good personal reasons, such as to relocate with their spouse, child-care, lack of transportation, care of a sick relative or friend, didn't like the employer or the work and any other personal reason, these would not meet the requirements necessary to pay benefits.

While this sounds reasonable, it's not what happens in the real world. Time and time again employers tell me how well they have documented the employee's misconduct only to have the state award unemployment benefits anyway. The manager of a restaurant lost a claim for unemployment benefits after firing an employee who stole money from the cash register. The employee was awarded the benefit because the restaurant had no written policy against embezzlement. Another company caught an employee using and selling marijuana at work. The employee was taken to a hospital where he was given a drug test that proved he had been smoking marijuana. The state still awarded him unemployment benefits because the employer did not have proof the hospital was certified to do drug testing. States are even paying unemployment benefits to employees who aren't fired, but who voluntarily quit their jobs.

Your chances of winning a claim are often pure chance, depending on the personality of the individual who is assigned to your case. I have found no simple solution to this horrific problem. However, you should take some basic steps. First, "Document, document, document!" An employee's handwritten personal improvement plan is one of the best documents you can provide. When he was put on decision-making leave and wrote suggestions to salvage his job, he essentially gave you a written confession of guilt. The most creative solution I've heard came from a manager in Chattanooga, Tennessee. He took photographs of help-wanted signs at area fast-food restaurants and picked up job applications from each one. He mailed the photographs and job applications to the department of employment security and his former employee. Because one of the criteria for receiving unemployment compensation is that the individual must be actively seeking employment, this worked to his advantage.

Another approach is to offer to rehire the employee. If he refuses employment, he disqualifies himself from unemployment benefits.

## Conclusion

If you lose the case, exhaust all your appeals. The time it will cost you will exceed the money you would have paid in SUTA taxes. It's still worth it. The frustration of a former employee who lies and gets rewarded for it will cause you more stress than any amount of money could justify. Having said that, business is business. Unemployment insurance is not that expensive in most states with low wage bases. It is not sufficient reason to keep a bad employee.

No matter how much your problem employees deserve to be fired, how well you document your case, or how many warnings you give, the day will come when you lose a claim for unemployment benefits despite your best efforts. You will feel defeated, powerless, and angry. The questions managers most often ask me in this situation is "Where's the justice in this?" There is no justice when unemployment benefits are wrongly awarded. The question managers should ask themselves is, "Did I do everything I should have done?" If you can answer yes, you have won the battle you have control over winning. Doing your best is the most you should expect of yourself. Fight it as best as you can and then move on to bigger battles. In the last chapter, we look at how to win many of those battles.

# CHAPTER 11

# How to Handle Daily Challenges Problem Employees Create

You've defined boundaries, hired the right people, protected yourself legally, and created a healthy work environment. You have a basic working knowledge of labor laws, behavioral psychology, and human resources. You've done everything you can do to be proactive. You are now more well rounded than most managers in the workforce today. It's time to do battle by putting it all into practice to solve the little problems that plague managers everywhere. What follows is a compilation of issues I am asked about most often in my seminars.

## Bad Attitudes

The problem with an employee who has a bad attitude is that her performance may seem good enough to outweigh her attitude, but this may not be the case. You have a bigger problem than attitude when your reaction to seeing her car in the parking lot is, "Darn, she's here again." When a manager is glad that an employee is absent, it's time to face facts: Something needs to be done and you're the person to do it. The great irony is that these people usually have good attendance. They enjoy coming to work because they're allowed to spew their venom until they get it out of their system.

People with bad attitudes tend to be good at their jobs because no employer would keep them if they weren't. Still, the morale of the entire company is more important than any one person within the company. A great receptionist who makes people's skin cringe is not a great receptionist. Build your case with specifics as we did in the example of the bartender in Chapter 2. Then confront the employee when you have a case you can win. You cannot force her to have a pleasant personality, but you can force her to be polite.

## Bad Bosses

Sometimes the problem employee is your boss. Part of being an assertive manager is holding everyone, including superiors, accountable for inappropriate behavior. The difference lies in how you approach the matter. Because you have authority over your employees, you can enforce policies even if they don't agree with the policies. Because you don't have authority over your boss, you can only make suggestions to him. He may not listen, but you have an obligation to give him the chance. We all need people to let us know when we are making mistakes.

First, let's look at the boss who nitpicks. You're good at what you do, but your boss never notices. He does, however, notice everything you do wrong. Pretend you work in property management. You finished a 200-page proposal a day early. He then called the customer and moved the presentation up by a day. He was able to get the customer to sign an $8 million lease because your quick turnaround allowed him to present his proposal before the competition presented theirs. He praised you by saying, "Great job! Next time use a size 10 typeface instead of a size 12 and it will be perfect." What a jerk. It is very likely that he does not see his behavior the way you do. He probably wouldn't have said it if he knew how it sounded. Maybe he sees it as fine-tuning, and doesn't realize the damage he's doing. It's your job to show him. The next time this happens, ask him what you did right. When he points out that you finished the proposal early, ask him what the benefit was. He's probably a perfectionist who is focusing on an irrelevant detail. He needs to broaden his tunnel vision to see that you helped him bring in $8 million.

Next, let's look at an incompetent boss. Pretend his superior delegates an assignment to him. You know from past experience that your boss will screw it up and blame it on you. Delegate backward by assuming personal responsibility for the assignment. It's better to get the job done correctly and make both of you look good than to sit idly while he makes both of you look bad.

If you wish to get rid of your boss, be careful. Office politics cost more people their jobs than incompetence. If your boss's behavior is so outrageous that it calls for termination, go to your boss's superior. Ask to speak to her confidentially about a problem employee. Describe the behavior without revealing whom you're describing, and then ask if she agrees that the behavior warrants termination. If she does, then reveal it's your boss. She'll have to take it from there.

## Blaming Others

Blaming others is a way of avoiding personal accountability. This is not, however, the only reason people do it. It's sometimes just a knee-jerk reaction to jump to conclusions when things go wrong. People often blame the usual suspects before they evaluate all the facts because it requires less effort than thinking a situation through. Attendees sometimes arrive for a seminar at 7:30 A.M., thinking it begins at 8:00 A.M. I study their faces when I explain it starts at 9:00 A.M. They never say, "I misunderstood." Instead, they insist the brochure read 8:00 A.M. and pull it out to show me. After they realize the brochure reads 9:00 A.M., they apologize and accept blame for their own misunderstanding.

Recently, my bookkeeper received a nasty e-mail from a customer who ordered a book from my web site. She thought we charged her credit card three times and demanded that we fix it immediately. My bookkeeper called the customer's bank and discovered their web site was posting all charges three times, even though they were only processed once. If the customer had other charges on the card, they would have also shown up three times. I suspect that since my book was ordered online, she jumped to the conclusion that the Internet order must be the culprit.

Even when it's not an impulse, people can be quite adept at assigning blame. Some people blame everyone but themselves for their problems. They can get away with it everywhere else in their lives, but not at work. It's management's responsibility to hold people accountable for their actions. When someone wrongly assigns blame to another, he makes the mistake of seeing it as an all or nothing proposition. Personal injury lawyers win their cases by assigning fault in percentages. The jury ruled that Stella Liebeck was 20 percent at fault when she spilt hot McDonald's coffee in her lap. Take the same approach with your employee. Ask your employee who claims to be 100 percent innocent, "Are you saying there is not 1/10th of 1 percent chance you could bear any responsibility?" Then work forward with the concept of personal responsibility.

## Breaking the Chain of Command

Children are great at playing parents against each other. If a child doesn't like the answer Dad gives, she'll ask Mom. Employees can do the same thing. If they don't like your answer, they can go over your head to your boss. This demonstrates the employee's lack of respect for your authority. To stop the behavior, you need your boss's support.

For example, Jim is a new supervisor. One of his employees has a bone of contention to pick with him but never brings it to him. Instead, she goes straight to Susan, the company president. The employee says to Susan, "I have a problem with Jim." Susan brings the employee into her office. After hearing the story, Susan says, "I appreciate you bringing this to my attention, but I agree with Jim's decision." In addition to having an employee who broke the chain of command, Jim also has a boss who broke the chain of command. He must repair the broken link above him before repairing the broken link beneath him. He should thank Susan for her support, and then suggest that she handle the situation differently in the future. When his employee comes to her about a problem with Jim, Susan needs to ask if the employee has spoken to Jim. If not, Susan needs to say to the employee, "Jim is your supervisor, and he has my full support. Speak to him first." Susan must send the employee back down the chain of command. Authority comes from above. If the person above you doesn't give you the authority to do your job, you become a "Barney Fife" manager. Barney had a gun but only carried one bullet, which stayed in his pocket. If your boss micromanages like Jim's, your ammunition has been taken away.

I'm often asked how this works in companies with open-door management policies. It works fine. Open-door management doesn't mean an employee can bypass the entire system; it means an employee is allowed to continue up the chain of command until he finds resolution to his problem. Imagine what would happen if every one of Wal-Mart's 1.4 million employees called the president on the same day; the home office would shut down. Employees must follow the chain of command. Once your boss is on the same page with you, dealing with the employee is straightforward.

## Bringing Personal Problems to Work

It's natural to be less than 100 percent productive when your personal life is falling apart. The problem arises when people exploit the situation. Some people use every little problem of life as an excuse to avoid accountability at work. The best solution I've found is to tell the story of Fleetwood Mac's work ethic. The year was 1976. Keyboardist Christine McVie was going through a bitter divorce from her husband, bass player John McVie. Singer Stevie Nicks separated from her long-time companion and guitarist Lindsey Buckingham. Drummer Mick Fleetwood was divorcing his wife Jenny Boyd. Their lives were falling apart, but they didn't slack off. They put their personal problems aside long enough to record "Rumors," which became their most successful album.

Can you do your best work when you don't feel like it? As discussed in Chapter 8, doing your best when you don't feel like it is called professionalism. Tell this story to the next employee who doesn't want to leave his or her personal problems at home. Then tell your employee you will accept nothing less from him or her.

## Camping Out in the Restroom

The restroom is the only private place in the office where employees can hide. They can check personal voice mail, send text messages, read, smoke, or just relax. Although it would be difficult to create a policy defining how long an employee is allowed to spend in the restroom, we do have some general guidelines. California, Colorado, Kentucky, Nevada, and Washington require a paid 10-minute rest period for each four consecutive hours of work. Minnesota requires, "a paid adequate rest period to utilize the nearest convenient restroom for each four consecutive hours of work," although they don't specify how long the break must be. While you can't restrict how long an employee stays in the restroom, you can make it a less attractive place to hang out. Create a written policy that prohibits smoking, eating, reading, text messaging, or making phone calls in the restroom. Don't allow magazines or newspapers to be taken in. The restroom is to be used only for the toilet facilities. Some companies have even removed doors from the stalls to make them less private. One company installed a large clock on the wall to keep people conscious of how long they've been in the restroom. Another installed motion-activated lights that go off after 10 minutes without activity. The sensor is located so that an employee can wave his arm to reactivate it. It's a subtle way of reminding him how long he's been in there. The most radical method is to disconnect the heating and air conditioning vent. When the temperature is uncomfortable, people will spend less time in there.

## Carelessness

The dictionary defines carelessness as "failure to act with the prudence that a reasonable person would exercise under the same conditions." Some employees are careful and exercise great caution in everything they do. They pay attention to detail but are slower than others. Attention to detail and speed have an inverse relationship. An employee's quality of work decreases as the quantity of work increases. This is why speed demons accomplish more but make more mistakes. When an employee is making too many mistakes, look for the cause. It may be that he needs to slow down. Slowing him down and requiring him to check his work is easy. The more difficult situation arises when it's a personality trait. If not caring is the problem, focus on the performance instead of the behavior. Telling an employee she is careless is too broad of a problem to solve, and she may think you're nitpicking. Be specific by pointing out what she is doing wrong and helping her understand why accuracy matters.

## Cell Phones

Bringing a cell phone to work is not a right; it's a privilege. Privileges are given only when employees don't abuse them. Once they are abused, privileges are revoked. Cell phones invite disruption in the workplace. Decide how much of this privilege you will allow. Some companies don't allow employees to have cell phones in the workplace. Others allow cell phones only if it stays on silent alert. If it rings once, the employee receives a warning. If it rings again, the employee permanently loses the privilege. Some employees argue that it's their personal cell phone. This may be true, but it's your time. You bought it from them. Prior to 2001, companies were leaning toward prohibiting personal cell phones at work. When panicked children couldn't reach their parents on 9/11, many companies eased up on the restriction. They tightened it again in 2003 because of camera phones, which pose additional problems. A conventional camera can be confiscated before film is developed or photos downloaded, but camera phones allow a photo to be e-mailed immediately. Daimler Chrysler and General Motors prohibit camera phones in certain facilities to protect trade secrets. The Oakland County Courthouse near Detroit does not allow camera phones out of concern that an undercover agent could be photographed and his life could be put in jeopardy. A more common problem is sexual harassment if an employee inappropriately photographs coworkers. A survey by the Society for Human Resource Management revealed 40 percent of organizations had a written policy on cell phone usage.[1] An additional 12 percent planned to implement policies within the year. If your company doesn't already have a cell phone policy, now is a good time to consider one.

## Character and Integrity

The importance of character and integrity in business can't be overstated. In 1902, President Theodore Roosevelt's attorney general, Philander Knox, held public hearings to break J. P. Morgan's monopoly on railroads. Morgan was so wealthy that he personally saved the United States from near insolvency twice. When he stated that he placed a higher value on character and integrity than money in his business dealings, Knox asked how this could be possible for such a wealthy man. Morgan responded, "If a man does not have character and integrity, he won't get any of my money."

Whether you're a billionaire like Morgan or a new supervisor, it's helpful to know if your employees have integrity. Because none of us are above temptation, we don't know what our true character or level of integrity is until we're faced with temptation. Values are useless unless someone has the strength and commitment to abide by them when tempted. One business owner tested an employee under suspicion by dropping a $100 bill in the employee's chair. When the employee said nothing, the owner announced in the next company meeting that he was missing $100 from the deposit and thought he may have dropped it. When the employee remained silent, the owner knew where to focus his attention. He eventually discovered the employee had embezzled $60,000. Hire for character and integrity, and train for skill.

## Cheating on Time Sheets

I call time sheets the "Otis Campbell" time clock. Otis was the town drunk on *The Andy Griffith Show.* Andy left the jail cell keys hanging on the wall so Otis could let himself out when he sobered up. This honor system may have worked in Mayberry, but it doesn't work in the real world. Having people fill out their own time sheets defeats the purpose. Some managers argue their employees are honest and would never fudge the numbers. It's not the honest ones that concern me. The dishonest employee who cheats on his time sheet is the reason we need time clocks. If your organization is too small to justify buying one, you can download a virtual time clock on the Internet. Go to www.download.com and type "time clock" in the search field.

## Chronic Arguing

Arguing is not always a bad thing. Just as with rebellion, there's a proper time, place, and way to argue. If you're falsely accused of a crime, you want your lawyer to argue fervently and convincingly. Chronic arguers do it for the wrong reason, or no reason at all. Arguing is as immediate of an impulse for them as jerking a finger back from a hot iron.

Military strategists know they must have an exit strategy when entering a conflict. They must plan ahead by defining what constitutes victory. Chronic arguers lack the discretion to discern which arguments can't be won. They want to win every argument, but end up losing most of them. On July 4, 2002, an Egyptian gunman began firing randomly in Los Angeles International Airport (LAX). He killed two Israeli nationals and wounded four others. Authorities nationwide went on high alert because they thought this might signal the next wave of terrorist attacks. I had just landed at LAX as the bullets were flying. It was the closest I've ever been to a terrorist attack. I didn't see the shooting because I was in the domestic terminal, and the attack occurred in the international terminal. As I left the airport in a taxi, I saw LAPD helicopters overhead. I assumed it was standard security for the holiday, having no idea what just happened. I later discovered the airport closed for eight hours and detained over 15,000 passengers just as I was leaving. I literally got out in the nick of time. About 30 minutes later, I checked into my hotel in Beverly Hills. The front desk clerk asked how I got to LA from Nashville. I told him I had a direct flight into LAX on Southwest Airlines. He responded, "You couldn't have." I asked what he meant, and he explained there had been a terrorist attack and the airport closed. I said, "I don't know what to tell you. I just flew in from Nashville and everything seemed fine." He retorted, "That's just not possible!" "Fine," I said, "I walked to California from Tennessee!

Now can I please check in to my room?" This guy didn't understand that his argument couldn't be won, even if I were willing to lose. The only way he could have won the argument was to change the events of the day. Can you imagine him working in customer service at your company?

Other times an argument can be won, but it simply isn't going to happen. Some people just don't want to accept this reality. About once a year, a seminar attendee with an entitlement mentality pitches a fit because my books and CDs are a separate purchase item. She demands to know why I don't give them away free. My standard answer is, "For the same reason movie theaters don't give away free popcorn, Circuit City doesn't give away free extended warranties, and the Rolling Stones don't give away free CDs at their concerts. This is how I make my living." She then goes on to tell me about some seminar she attended that gave away free books. At this point, I end the discussion. The question was asked and answered. I don't bother to explain that neither Fred Pryor, CareerTrack, Dun & Bradstreet, Padgett-Thompson, Zig Ziglar, Tony Robbins, Deepak Chopra, Brian Tracy, Wayne Dyer, Stephen Covey, Tom Peters, or anyone else in the business gives away their products for free. This would defeat the concept of capitalism. I also don't bother to explain what an insult it is to expect me to give away a product I work all hours of the night, on weekends, and through holidays to write. I can whip a speech out of thin air and address a live audience at a moment's notice. Writing a book takes months and sometimes years. She doesn't want to hear this because it's reason. Chronic arguers don't respond to reason. They don't want to hear the real answer to their questions; they just want to argue.

Winning is a victory for one person, but peace is a victory for both. For chronic arguers, winning is more important than peace. Hence, placing a higher value on winning than on peace destroys relationships. This is why chronic arguers don't go far in careers or in life. A wise person knows compromise can sometimes be more beneficial than an all out victory. If Benjamin Franklin had not understood this, there would be no United States of America. Representatives from the original 13 colonies couldn't stop arguing over how a legislative body should be created. Large states like Virginia wanted representation by population. Small states like Rhode Island wanted the same number of votes as the large states. They were about to give up hope when Mr. Franklin suggested a bicameral legislature. All states would have two senators while the seats in Congress were tied to each state's population.

Employees should be allowed to disagree as long as they do it in a civil manner. Intel in Santa Clara, California, encourages people to disagree but prohibits personal attacks. Do the same with your employees. Disagreements are fine. Arguing and personal attacks are not.

## Chronic Complaining and Whining

There is a huge difference between complaining and whining. Sometimes complaining can be productive. When citizens complain enough to the city traffic department about a dangerous intersection, a stop sign will eventually be erected. When complaining is pointless, it becomes whining. Complaining about the rain would be whining because no amount of complaining will make the sun appear. However, whining can be therapeutic for the whiner. He'll feel better after whining, but now you're as miserable as he was. He just metaphorically rained on your day. Therapists are paid to listen to people's problems—you're not.

In keeping with our mantra of being fair, we must be sure the employee is aware of what he's doing. Chances are good that no one's ever taken the time to explain the damage his whining does to his career and his relationships. You now get to play Dr. Phil and the employee gets one pass. The next time he whines about something like the rain, call him aside and explain the difference between complaining and whining. Then ask, "How do you think I feel after you tell me about the same weather I drove through?" Conclude with "I would appreciate it if you only shared problems I might have some reasonable ability to solve." The next time he whines, politely say, "Remember the conversation we had?" Never ask a whiner "What do you expect me to do about it?" This phrase sounds sarcastic, even though you may not mean it that way.

The situation changes with problems you can solve. It is easier for an employee to ask you to solve her problem for her than for her to solve it herself. A weak manager will keep his office door closed to hide from employees who constantly interrupt him with "I've got a problem." It's unwise to prevent employees from coming to you with all problems. Managers need to know what's going on, without enabling employees to become dependent on them for a solution to every problem. When she informs you she has a problem, don't give her the opportunity to ramble on until it turns into whining. If this has been the pattern, respond with "Give me the *Reader's Digest* version of it. Tell me what the problem is in two sentences or less." After she tells you, respond with "What do you suggest we do about it?" Teach your employees to find a solution to their own problems. It doesn't have to be a good solution, but she has to come up with something. After she offers up a solution, respond with "That sounds like a great plan. In case it doesn't work, what's your backup plan?" There's usually one obvious solution to most problems. Asking for a second solution forces her to think harder. Eventually she'll realize it's easier to solve problems on her own than to bring them to you. Then the ones she'll bring to you will be the ones she can't solve on her own, which are ones you need to hear.

## Company Charge Card Abuse

Spending other people's money is addictive. It's sometimes called OPM, and it may truly be as addictive as the narcotic opium. Providing company charge cards is asking for trouble because there's no accountability. Even the federal government faces this problem with its employees. There are 1.4 million government-sponsored credit cards. Employees have been caught using them for personal expenses including alcohol, prostitution, and gambling. An investigation of 300 of the Department of Agriculture's credit cards found $7.7 million in personal purchases in a six-month period. Department of Defense employees have failed to repay more than $60 million in personal charges on federal credit cards since 1998.

Companies have no idea what employees are purchasing when debit or credit card charges aren't audited. I am a prime example. I travel extensively and carry a card just for gas, hotels, rental cars, and airline tickets. When I fuel up at a gas station, I might also buy a six-pack of diet Coke. My bookkeeper has no way of knowing the charge was for anything other than gas. It presents no problem for me since I own the company. If I didn't, I could easily defraud my employer by claiming I only purchased gas.

My first advice on company charge cards is not to provide them. Require employees to pay for everything out of their own pockets and then file for reimbursement on an expense voucher. This will decrease how much they spend and eliminate charge card abuse. If you insist on giving your employees company charge cards, require itemized store receipts for each purchase. Then hold employees personally liable for any charges when a receipt is not provided.

## Company Vehicle Misuse

Think back to when you received your first driver's license at 16. The right to drive gave you freedom and independence. The same is true with employees. Company vehicles give employees unlimited independence, which can open the door for abuse. No matter how honest an employee might be, a company car is more tempting than a company charge card. He has unsupervised freedom during business hours. Technology offers a solution with Global Positioning Systems (GPS). A GPS allows the employer to view a map on the Internet and see exactly where the vehicle is, how fast it's going, or how long it's been parked. The manager of a car dealership in Georgia told me their fuel bill dropped by 28 percent after they installed GPSs on their parts delivery trucks. A manager in Ohio installed GPSs after discovering his employee robbed a bank in a company truck while on lunch break.

Regardless of whether you monitor where employees go in company vehicles, you need a written policy spelling out specifics of how the vehicle should be operated. Examples include:

No talking on a cell phone while driving.

Seat belts must be worn at all times while in a moving vehicle.

Observe and comply with all traffic regulations.

Keep a current driver's license.

Notify the company of traffic citations you receive, whether in a company vehicle or your own.

Stop at all railroad crossings.

Should your employee be involved in a traffic accident, these policies could deter a lawsuit against you for negligent management practices.

## Conflicts between Coworkers

When one good employee is paired with another, we don't always get two good employees. Sometimes we get two bad employees. It may be that neither has done anything wrong; they might just rub each other the wrong way. This is when managers need to resolve conflict between coworkers.

Imagine Vickie and Susan can't get along. They're constantly at each other's throats. You can't leave them unsupervised for two minutes without a confrontation erupting. Intervene by mediating. Bring them into your office and have them sit in chairs facing each other. Ask Vickie to tell her side of the story. Notice the implication is that there are two sides to the story. Each assumes she is 100 percent right and the other is 100 percent wrong. Vickie proceeds to tell her story. No holds are barred, so you must maintain control of the situation. Vickie accuses Susan of coming to work intoxicated, using drugs, and a myriad of other unsavory things. No matter how much she exaggerates, let her get it out all of her system. You'll know she's finished when she sighs, which indicates she got it all off her chest. This is already a small victory, because chances are good that neither employee had a chance to complete a sentence while at each other's throats. Now it's Susan's turn. She slashes Vickie into 1,000 pieces. Listen quietly until she gets to her sigh. You have now completed step one in the mediation process. Both parties have spoken their piece.

Now make a list of their disagreements, removing the personal attacks and boiling them down to objective facts. Imagine Vickie accused Susan of being an idiot on the computer. Susan defended herself by pointing out she simply prefers WordPerfect while Vickie prefers Microsoft Word. Write this down on your list. When you finish the points on which they disagree, make a list of points on which they do agree. Start by saying "Susan, you prefer WordPerfect and Vickie prefers Microsoft Word. We disagree on the word processing program, but can we agree it would be helpful if everyone uses the same program?" Write, "Need to standardize on one word processing program" as your first point of agreement. Then continue down the list. If you're unable to find anything they agree on, they can at least agree to disagree without personal attacks. You are now defining another boundary. When you're finished, make a closing statement such as "It looks like we have the same goals. We just have different ideas on how to achieve them." Now go through the list and find common ground. You may need to establish new policies or procedures as a result of your mediation process. The office manager of a law firm in Mississippi supervised two file clerks who had it in for each other. They were constantly stepping in each other's territory. She sat down with both, and told them no one was leaving the room until they worked it out. She ended up dividing the alphabet in half. One took the first half and the other took the second. After that, they were fine together.

## Crying

Crocodile tears are an easy way to avoid reprimand. If you stop a disciplinary conversation while an employee cries, she learns it works. You just became the mother who gave the little girl the doll at the toy store. Any time your employee wants to avoid a disciplinary conversation in the future, she will cry. The solution is to hand her a tissue and continue the conversation.

## Cyber Loafing

Personal phone calls were the biggest time killer in the workplace 10 years ago. The amount of time wasted on the phone today pales in comparison to time wasted on personal e-mail and surfing the Internet. In *Managing Your E-mail: Thinking Outside the Inbox*, Christina Cavanaugh estimates the cost of excessive e-mail is 12 percent of annual payroll.[2] Cyber loafing is the term for employees who surf the Internet or send and read e-mail when they should be working. You would never allow an employee to have a television on his desk, make dozens of personal phone calls each day, shop through catalogs, and browse *Playboy* magazine. Yet, this is what people are doing via the Internet. Personal computers were office machines in the 1980s. They are now toys as well. The problem of employees playing solitaire was easy to solve; companies simply removed it from all computers. Cyber loafing is a little trickier. DuPont monitors employees' Internet usage. Employees of one energy company are blocked from certain Internet sights. If they attempt to access those sights, a message pops up on their screen reminding them the computer is company property. When Pillsbury employees send e-mail, a note flashes on their screen reminding them to watch what they send.

A less obvious but more expensive potential consequence of cyber loafing is the legal nightmare it can cause. A secretary at a California company sued her employer for $3.5 million for a hostile work environment after supervisors repeatedly downloaded pornography. The company offered $850,000 to settle, but she declined. Medical professionals now monitor outgoing e-mail to ensure no patient information is given out in violation of HIPPA. The financial sector monitors outgoing e-mail to guard against SEC violations. Goldman Sachs paid $2 million to federal regulators for employees' improper use of e-mail. Merrill Lynch banned employee use of AOL and Yahoo e-mail.

A study published by the American Management Association found that over half of U.S. companies monitor employees' e-mail, 75 percent have written policies concerning e-mail, and 22 percent have terminated employees for e-mail infractions.[3] Monitoring software can be downloaded by going to www.download.com and typing "e-mail monitoring" or "Internet monitoring" in the search field.

## Dropping the Ball

Some people are doers while others are just big talkers. This is one of the dilemmas in interviewing job applicants. The applicant who can sell anything to anybody in the interview turns out to be useless once he's hired. I meet plenty of these big talkers on planes. It seems half the people I sit beside tell me they're writing a book. I give them my card and tell them I'd love an autographed copy. I have yet to receive one. The old adage is that losers always find an excuse, while winners find a way to get things done.

Other people are good at taking initiative, but lousy at following through. I once used an attorney like this. He didn't return my calls and frequently dropped the ball. He also changed firms numerous times. Needless to say, he lost me as a client. Steve Underwood is the opposite. He is bombarded with thousands of requests for information each year. Yet, when I asked him for information, he responded promptly. Steve is an attorney for the Tennessee Titans. He's a get-it-done kind of guy. Kaye LeFebvre of Mojave, California, receives even more requests than Steve. Hers come from all over the world. Yet when I asked for information on her company, she also responded promptly. She works for Scaled Composites, the small company that made history by putting the first private manned vehicle into space. Kaye and Steve have limited staffs, but both get the job done. No wonder they work for such impressive organizations. Another organization I contacted for information in researching this book has a much larger staff, but hasn't responded to my requests months after I submitted them. That organization is the U.S. Department of Labor. I also meet numerous people who can't follow through in academia. Doctoral candidates often complete their classes but never complete their dissertation. Instead of PhDs, we call them ABDs. This stands for "all but dissertation."

The solution for employees who drop the ball is twofold. First, set the tone for your company. Do you want to be like the federal government, or like the company that won a $10 million prize for putting the first private manned vehicle into space? You don't pay employees to talk about what they're going to do. You don't pay them to tell you why it can't be done. You pay them to get it done. Teach your employees to be proactive. Pay them $100 each to read Stephen Covey's *The 7 Habits of Highly Effective People*.[4] Instill the "Where there's a will, there's a way" mentality in them. Eat it, drink it, live it. Teach them to see things through to the end. The second step is to practice this yourself. Follow-up, follow-up, follow-up. All employees can learn to get things done and see projects through to the end. Some just need strong management to teach them the habit. Managers are ultimately responsible for employees' work habits, good or bad.

## English as a Second Language

Millions of legal immigrants in this country hold legitimate jobs but speak little English. Employers in California, Florida, and Texas often send their managers to classes to learn Command Spanish. This is very simple crash course that law enforcement officers take. It teaches the minimum required words to communicate basic messages. When this is not possible, a short-term solution is a telephone-based interpretation service. Companies such as AT&T offer interpretation services for virtually any language. This was introduced for the 1996 Olympics and provides a valuable tool for employers in today's multicultural society. The employee and supervisor talk into a speakerphone or two telephone extensions while an unbiased operator translates. Some companies will even provide transcripts of conversations.[5]

## Eating at One's Desk

Would you have a problem with an employee who drinks a cup of coffee at her desk? What if she orders a pizza for delivery and works through her lunch hour? These would certainly be reasonable. The problem occurs when she keeps a two-liter bottle of Pepsi, a jumbo size bag of Doritos, and a half-eaten candy bar at her workstation throughout the day. Her computer keys have a greasy orange hew from her food stained fingertips. Spills and cup rings cover her desk. Where do you draw the line? This is another boundary issue. Some companies limit food items to one at a time, while others totally prohibit eating at workstations. Still other companies provide free unlimited snacks and soft drinks for their employees. Most companies have no written policy on eating while working. Just because it's not in writing, however, doesn't mean they don't have a policy. The absence of a written policy implies it's okay to eat whatever an employee wants to eat, whenever he or she wants to eat. As long as this does not create a problem and productivity doesn't suffer, the implied policy works. Once the eating becomes a problem, it's time to create a more specific policy and put it in writing.

## Employee Theft

John Case, president of a security management-consulting firm, says, that employees steal to the extent management permits it. A 1999 survey by forensic accounting firm Michael G. Kessler & Associates revealed that 79 percent of workers admit they have or would consider stealing from their employers. At every seminar, I ask how many managers have caught employees stealing from them. About one-third consistently raise their hands. When an employee embezzles, the issue is actually simpler to deal with than when an employee is caught slipping a bottle of Liquid Paper into his pocket. Employees should be terminated for theft. The difficulty sometimes lies in defining what constitutes theft. Does an employee get fired for walking out with a company ink pen in his pocket? You don't want to fire him for stealing a 39-cent office item. You probably couldn't prove he stole it anyway. At the same time, you have to do something about the problem if it's ongoing.

Sometimes it becomes more prudent to stop the behavior than to punish the offender. If you're not concerned about recovering the item and just want to stop the behavior, address it without singling anyone out. Send everyone a memo that reads, "I know someone's been stealing Liquid Paper. There's a $100 reward for whoever turns him or her in first." He'll become paranoid and start looking over his shoulder. For $100, people will turn in their own children and parents.

## Excessive Personal Phone Calls

An online poll conducted jointly by the Society for Human Resource Management and CareerJournal.com[6] indicated that 42 percent of HR professionals who responded reported occasionally monitoring employee telephone use. The oldest monitoring method is recording the calls. The federal wiretapping act allows employers to record employees' phone calls as long as the call is on a company extension phone and "in the ordinary course of its business." What legally constitutes the ordinary course of business is murky. So to be safe, inform everyone you'll be recording. The federal law allows recording of personal and business calls on a company extension as long as the employee has given consent. Consent does not need to be explicit. It can also include acquiescence to a known system. Always check with your attorney to be sure.

A newer and easier monitoring method is call accounting software. Programs such as Call Tarifficator (www.dcslab.net) and Phonestat (www.vocaltechsoft.com) provide written reports of all incoming and outgoing calls by extension, date, time, and phone number. As with recording calls, check with your attorney before installing call accounting software. While there are generally no legal restrictions on this, state laws constantly change.

## Extramarital Affairs between Employees

Extramarital affairs between employees bring up a different dilemma than office romances between unmarried adults. Disregarding the ethics side, the employer faces potential legal problems. When unmarried coworkers are dating, they'll be more likely to curtail affection at work because they can see each other outside the office. When one or both are married, the office may be their only rendezvous point. This creates a possible hostile work environment for the employer. It may also put coworkers in an uncomfortable position. An employee of Home Depot in Colorado walked in on a sexual encounter between his store manager and a coworker. He then filed a claim for a hostile work environment. It eventually mushroomed into a lawsuit by the EEOC, which was settled for $5.5 million. While we do not know the marital status of the individuals in this case, we do know everyone would have been better off if it had been kept out of the workplace.

Ross Perot will fire an executive caught cheating on his wife. When asked why, he is reported to have said, "If your wife can't trust you, how can I?" It would be difficult to institute a policy that prohibits fraternization between employees based on their marital status. Some companies will create a blanket policy that prohibits fraternization between all employees. Others celebrate legitimate relationships that began at work. Wal-Mart allows weddings of employees who met at work to be held in their stores so that coworkers can attend. Humans will do what humans choose to do regardless of your policy. Having a policy in place will help legally protect you should things turn ugly.

## Falsifying Expense Reports or Mileage Logs

The first problem with falsifying expense reports or mileage logs is evidenced in the fact that we refer to it as falsifying instead of cheating, lying, or stealing. It has somehow been watered down to seem more acceptable. It is not acceptable. Managers should view it as theft, and create a policy explaining the consequence. Lying on a mileage log or expense report isn't the problem; it's the symptom. The problem is the individual's character and integrity. Character and integrity in business are paramount to success. When an employee demonstrates he can't be trusted, some form of accountability must be implemented. A GPS is the ultimate solution for cheating on mileage logs. If you're not this high tech, start with the basics. Periodically check the odometer to see if it corresponds with mileage logs. The key to preventing expense report fraud is to require itemized store receipts on everything. As discussed earlier in this chapter, never accept a charge card statement without an itemized store receipt. Once an employee has demonstrated that he can't be trusted, it is your responsibility to monitor him more closely than before.

## Foul Language

I realize that people utter expletives when they're surprised, angry, or in pain. When I hit my thumb with a hammer, I say things I wouldn't want my mother to hear. I'm also aware society has drastically lowered its standards regarding profanity in the past few decades. I remember when Jimmy Buffett first used "damn" in his 1977 hit "Margaritaville." It raised a ruckus with the local deejay, but he played the record. Lyrics in today's gangster rap make "Margaritaville" seem benign. In 1978, the U.S. Supreme Court upheld the Federal Communications Commission's (FCC) definition of the seven dirty words not allowed on television or radio. The FCC has since loosened up on two of those words.

I still dislike hearing people use certain words in casual conversation. It makes them sound tacky and low class. Debra Benton, author of *Executive Charisma*[7] and *How to Think Like a CEO*,[8] says women need to be especially cognizant of their language if they want to be promoted. She has interviewed nearly 100 male CEOs and asked what's holding back so many qualified women. Many say the women make the mistake of trying to be one of the boys with their language. She equates women using foul language at work to wearing outfits with necklines too low or hemlines too high. Dianna Durkin, president of Loyalty Factor, a consulting firm, says that the corporate world still expects women to speak properly.

Regardless of people's personal values or gender, foul language at work can cause problems for everyone. Managers must be fair and consistent in holding employees accountable. Because the federal government holds you legally accountable for your employees' language, you need a written policy against profanity and vulgarity. It defines a behavioral boundary and sets a standard for professionalism. It can also help in your defense of a hostile work environment lawsuit.

## Friends

Supervising close friends rarely works because the dynamics of the two relationships contradict one another. Friendships are based on mutuality. Friends reveal intimate secrets to each other and make themselves vulnerable. Managers are in a one-up, one-down relationship with their subordinates. It is not possible to simultaneously be a person's superior and his equal. Either your friendship or your ability to supervise will suffer. The average job lasts about three years, but a good friend lasts a lifetime. Good employees are easier to find than good friends, so don't hire your friends.

The situation differs if you developed a friendship with coworkers who were previously your peers, and you've recently become their supervisor. After-hours social outings are now different. If you regularly went out with your coworkers in the past, don't stop altogether. This will be too abrupt and they'll think becoming a manager has gone to your head. Start pulling back slowly by periodically finding an excuse to decline invitations. On the nights you do go, leave early so they can have fun without the boss. Once you become a manager, you're not one of them any more. Don't fool yourself into thinking differently.

## Gossiping

Gossipers don't gossip about people to their faces. They do it behind their backs. It is a prime example of passive-aggressive behavior. The key to ending gossip is to remember the greatest fear of passive-aggressive people is direct confrontation. Forcing a direct confrontation takes the fun out of gossiping. Imagine that Tammy walks into your office and says, "Did you hear what Brenda did this weekend?" You know it's just as wrong to listen to gossip as it is to spread it, and you need to stop the behavior. Don't respond, "I don't want to hear this. It sounds like gossip." She'll go find someone else to tell. Instead, respond with "I'm just dying to hear this, but wait one second while I call Brenda." Pick up the phone as if you are calling Brenda. Pretend she answers and say, "Can you please come to my office? Tammy wants to talk about you." Tammy will be gone before Brenda would have time to get to your office. Requiring a gossiper to confront her victim takes the fun out of it.

## Group Gripe Sessions

An employee who comes to you to discuss a problem in private is doing her duty. When five employees come to you to discuss a problem, it's an ambush. You can't have a conversation with five people at once. You're outnumbered and the situation can quickly spin out of control. Tell them you'll only meet with one at a time. Alternatively, you might tell them to choose a spokesperson and you'll meet with her. Allowing five disgruntled workers to commiserate creates a feeding frenzy, and the only meal on the platter is you. Don't put yourself in such a compromising position.

## Guns in the Workplace

A Pizza Hut near Indianapolis, Indiana, fired a deliveryman after he shot and killed an armed robber. The deliveryman had a permit to carry the weapon and was not charged after prosecutors decided he acted in self-defense. Pizza Hut fired him for violating their no weapons policy. He argued, "It's not fair. If I'm going to die, I'd rather be killed defending myself." How could anyone argue with that? It isn't fair. It also isn't clear what the right course of action would be. The U.S. Department of Labor reports one employee is killed and 25 seriously injured by impulse attacks in the workplace nearly every week. Employers do not want weapons readily available when these attacks occur.

I have mixed feelings on this issue. As a gun owner and member of the NRA, I cringe when people talk about restricting second amendment rights. As a business owner, I don't want my employees carrying guns. Some companies compromise by allowing employees to keep their weapons locked in their automobiles. Other companies forbid weapons anywhere on company property. An America Online call center near Salt Lake City, Utah, fired three employees who were caught with guns in their vehicles. They weren't on the clock and were planning to go target shooting after work. Since the parking lot was part of a public strip mall, the employees argued that AOL could not forbid them from having weapons in a public area. The Utah Supreme Court sided with AOL, noting that employers have the right to ban guns, even in parking lots. Your policy could help protect you legally should a shooting occur. More importantly, it could save lives by preventing an impulse attack. There is no clear answer, so choose your battle wisely.

## High-Maintenance Employees

Athletes and rock stars are often high maintenance. As long as they are high producers, companies will invest in them. They eventually come to a point of diminishing returns. Country music legend George Jones faced this when his drinking and lack of dependability became so bad that he earned the nickname "No-Show Jones." Ostentatious basketball player Dennis Rodman was extremely high maintenance. He was also the leading rebounder in the NBA for seven seasons. Eventually his high maintenance personality exceeded his athletic talent and he found himself out of basketball. He wanted to make a comeback at age 43, but had difficulty finding a team who wanted him. He was quoted as saying, "They think I'm uncoachable and I don't know why." Rodman's bad reputation outlasted his value in the marketplace.

When we pay a premium for something, we expect a premium return on investment. Just as there is salary creep, there is maintenance creep. As long as an employee's productivity justifies his high maintenance, it's reasonable to tolerate it. As soon as the hassle of managing an employee exceeds his value, he needs to go.

## Hypochondriacs

Hypochondriacs are people who always think they're sick. Imagine you greet someone with, "How are you today?" and he responds by telling you how his hemorrhoids have been acting up. That's more information then you really wanted. Hypochondriacs have learned how to get attention by eliciting sympathy. It's not a healthy form of attention, but it's attention nonetheless. People resort to this when they can't get attention through healthier means such as being interesting, fun, or pleasant. Hypochondriac employees want you to feel sympathy for them and allow them do less work. When one tells you how sick he is, respond, "If you need time off, go home and recover. If you're going to stay at work, I need 100 percent from you." He will usually decline to go home, particularly if he already used his sick days. If he stays, give him extra work to do. When he whines again about a sickness he really doesn't have, give him even more work to do. Eventually he'll realize that instead of allowing him to do less work, his hypochondria is forcing him to do more. He will have the most miraculous recovery you've ever seen.

Sometimes the hypochondriac runs out of his own suffering and exploits someone else's. He always knows someone who's sick, dead, or dying. He'll come in Monday and tell you who died over the weekend. I sometimes wonder if these people spend the weekend reading obituaries. If he's truly in mourning, let him leave work and mourn. If he stays at work, he has to do his job. Sometimes people will twist this so far that they exploit their pet's sickness to elicit sympathy. I call it "Munchausen's Syndrome by Puppy." Don't fall for it; hold everyone accountable.

## Indecisiveness

Passive people don't like to make decisions. Imagine that you invite one to lunch. You ask where she wants to eat and she responds, "I don't care." You choose a local Tex-Mex restaurant, but she quips, "Their food is too spicy for my system." You ask her again where she wants to eat, but she still won't choose. It will drive you batty just trying to get to lunch. The old therapist's joke is that two passive people should never marry or they'll starve to death. The same thing happens when an employer asks an indecisive employee a direct question. Pretend you're an electrical contractor. You say to Bob, your foreman, "The general contractor wants to know if we're going to finish wiring this out by Friday. Are we?" Bob is passive and terrified of conflict. He knows if he answers yes and then misses the deadline, conflict will occur Friday. If he answers no and confesses he's a day behind schedule, conflict occurs now. Instead, he answers, "I don't know." This is his way of avoiding accountability. The problem is that you pay him to know. Teach him that a wrong answer is better than no answer. Look him squarely in the eye and say, "Well if you did know, what would your answer be?" Don't budge an inch until he answers.

Another approach to managing indecisive employees is to make their decisions for them, but make choices they won't like. Imagine you need Beverly to help plan the company Christmas party. You give her a choice of tasks, but she won't decide. She is extremely shy, and would prefer to mail out invitations rather than deal with caterers. Because she won't make a decision, give her the worst task you can think of. Have her address the entire company and welcome them to the Christmas party. Public speaking is the most common fear and is especially terrifying for shy people. Beverly will learn to make her own choices in the future.

## Insubordination

Self-employed people like to do things their way. The editor of *Entrepreneur* magazine says entrepreneurs are the only people who can go from sheer exhilaration to sheer terror, and back again every 24 hours. I'm one of those people. I would rather go broke doing it my way than get rich doing it the way someone else tells me. I haven't had a weekly paycheck since 1988, and I like it like that. I enjoy being a maverick and taking risks. I also know I have to submit to the authority figures in my life. When I'm the pilot in command of a Cessna 172 and the air traffic controller says "Skyhawk Four Sierra Papa, descend to 3,000 feet and fly a heading of 270," I must comply completely. The consequences can be serious if I don't. The tower chief can report me to the FAA and I could lose my pilot's license. I could also endanger other aircraft by deviating just a few degrees. I respect the air traffic controller's authority because I understand the consequences if I don't.

If you think insubordination at work isn't as serious as a pilot who doesn't follow assigned flight vectors, think again. Authorities are now bringing criminal charges against supervisors for accidental employee deaths. According to OSHA, at least eight supervisors have been criminally prosecuted for allowing violation of safety rules that resulted in an employee's death. Are you willing to go to prison because your employees didn't follow the rules? When rules are not followed, people can get hurt. Ask anyone who works in an industrial setting how difficult it is to get employees to follow safety rules. Ordering an employee to wear a hairnet sounds like nagging until her hair gets caught in a meat grinder. It then becomes the wisdom of sages. Even in an office setting, lives can be put in jeopardy when employees don't follow rules. One common problem in doctors' offices is receptionists who diagnose patients over the phone. The receptionist obviously isn't qualified to diagnose anyone. Even if she were an MD, she would not diagnose patients over the phone. While the receptionist might see this as being helpful, the results can be disastrous. She could cause the doctor to lose his license or patients to lose their lives.

Employees are insubordinate when they don't respect the manager's authority. They don't respect the manager's authority because the manager allows it. This happens when a manager tolerates too much bad behavior. It also happens when a manager shows too many signs of weakness. The solution is to stop doing both. No matter how long people have run roughshod over the boss, they can always change. They will not change until the manager makes them. This is done by being firm, but fair and consistent. Set boundaries, create policies, and hold people accountable. Insubordination is not always deadly, but it is always destructive.

## Irresponsibility

The Insurance Institute for Highway Safety reports that 16-year-old drivers are involved in accidents nearly nine times more often than drivers 20 or over. This is commonly attributed as much to irresponsibility as to lack of driving experience. They have not driven long enough to appreciate the consequences of their actions. Even when personal safety is not at stake, there can still be financial consequences to an accident. Having a driver's license revoked can mean having no way to get to work, and losing a job. This isn't a problem for a 16-year-old who knows food will still be on the table. It's a financial nightmare for the worker who is supporting a family.

As we age, we become more responsible and learn not to take unnecessary risks. When people don't suffer consequences for their actions, they don't learn responsibility. They must feel some pain in order to appreciate the consequences of their actions. Pretend that Delilah is responsible for mailing the IRS Form 941 by January 30. She forgets and mails it on February 10. The IRS assesses your company a late fee and penalty of $231. Explain to Delilah you just invested $231 into training her. The next time it happens, she'll be paying for her own education. Once she feels the pain of $231 deducted from her paycheck, she'll never forget to mail the Form 941 again. If you were to do this, keep in mind that you may need to spread the deduction over several pay periods so it doesn't cause her check to dip below minimum wage.

## Know-It-Alls

The less successful people are, the more inclined they are to give unsolicited advice. People who can't run their own lives try to vicariously run the lives of others. People who are busy running their own lives don't have time to run anyone else's. A seminar attendee in Tulsa, Oklahoma, had a brilliant way of handling people like this. He knew that responding with "When I want your advice, I'll ask for it" only creates hostility. Instead, he challenges people by asking, "Why do you think your opinion matters to me?" This moves people from the offensive to the defensive, which takes away their power.

People I have never met sometimes try to tell me how to do my job. The less they know about it, the more inclined they are to tell me how to do it. Recently, in a seminar at a Massachusetts Holiday Inn, an attendee informed me it would look much better if coffee was provided. He then went on to tell me that Dun and Bradstreet served coffee at a recent seminar he attended. I asked how many people attended and he guessed about 20. There were 142 people attending mine. I asked why he thought we didn't serve coffee. He answered, "Because the company you work for is too cheap." I explained I own the company and had personally bought lunch for everyone attending the seminar as a marketing test. He apologized and then guessed, "Because the hotel ran out of coffee." He was so fixated on his coffee that he assumed there was something sinister about it not being served. I explained that when 142 people are saturated with coffee throughout a six-hour seminar, they'll be coming and going to the restrooms all day long. Doors will be slamming and people will be obstructing other's views as they walk in and out. He suggested that we needed to take more restroom breaks. Again, he demonstrated his ignorance. I explained that if 142 people attempt to use restrooms that can only handle six at a time, the chaos would be indescribable. During the afternoon break, he came back to inform me that there was a long line outside the ladies room and I might need to wait a few minutes before I started the final session of the seminar. All I could think was "Who made this guy a manager?" I put up with him because he was my customer. If he were my employee, the situation would have been different.

People who tell you how to do your job are giving unsolicited advice. When people give advice, it implies they are qualified to do so. You pay your attorney for legal advice. You pay your doctor for medical advice. You pay your CPA for accounting advice. These individuals are more educated and presumably more knowledgeable about their respective disciplines than you. They're in a one-up, one-down relationship with you when it comes to their subject matter.

Your attorney is in a position of power over you when it comes to matters of law because you have not studied or practiced law. This puts you in a subordinate position. You'd know better than to represent yourself if your attorney sued you.

Now imagine you're a professional tennis player, and your attorney is a mediocre player. He invites you to a game of tennis. You would now be in the superior position while he would shift to the subordinate position. At the end of the game, the two of you sit down to cool off. He brings up the case of an employee who is suing you and advises you how to proceed. In the blink of an eye, you and he have shifted roles again.

This is what happens when an employee tells you how to do your job. Normally you're in the superior position and he's your subordinate. As soon as he makes himself important enough to tell you how to do your job, he has usurped power from you. The problem for him is that it's phantom power. He's arrogant and lacks either awareness of or respect for boundaries. The problem for you is that you allowed it. The solution is to take control of the situation by asserting your real power. Reaffirm the positions of superior and subordinate. One way of achieving this is to use the universal comeback, "That's an inappropriate comment!"

Another way of handling know-it-alls is to make it obvious they're not as smart as they think. In the 1993 movie *Born Yesterday,* Melanie Griffith played a trophy wife who wasn't the sharpest tool in the shed. Her tycoon husband John Goodman had business with big wigs in Washington, DC, and didn't want her to embarrass him. He hired a college professor played by Don Johnson to tutor her.

Johnson realized she was a slow study, so he created a short cut. He taught her a fake-it-till-you-make-it approach to prepare her for a big dinner party. By making very general statements regarding the authority of the *Washington Post*, the United States being the policemen of a dangerous world, the price of being a super power, and the wisdom of Abraham Lincoln, she blended right in with all the senators and members of Congress. She didn't have a clue what she was talking about, but neither did they. In order to prove they were just as oblivious as she, Johnson taught her to mention how beneficial it would be if the UN would remove a specific amendment to a resolution. Everyone agreed. What only she and Johnson knew was that the amendment didn't exist. No one admitted they weren't familiar with the amendment. It was a modern portrayal of "The Emperor's New Clothes." Every time I hear know-it-alls blabbering about something they know nothing about, I picture Melanie Griffith in that movie and laugh out loud. I then challenge the know-it-all, by asking questions he or she probably can't answer. Examples are:

> How do you feel about Peter Drucker's statement that the Sarbanes-Oxley Act is ethically ambiguous?
>
> Do you think that WEP security for a WiFi network really provides the equivalent of wired protection?
>
> Do you think I use split infinitives too often?
>
> How do you feel about the SUTA wage base being raised?
>
> Do you think we should use RGB or CMYK colors on the TIFF files?
>
> What do you think a fair cap would be for Roth IRA contributions?

It puts them in their place every time. One manager asked what he should do if someone answered all the questions correctly. My response was "Promote him into management!"

## Lame Ducks

A lame duck usually refers to an elected official whose successor has already been elected but has not yet taken office. When a governor knows her political career will end in three months, she has no need to appease constituents. This is the only time politicians can truly vote their conscience. An employee who turns in his two-week notice becomes a lame duck. He has a new job lined up and no incentive to earn your approval during his last two weeks. He will be less than 100 percent in a best-case scenario, and could inflict serious damage to your company in a worst-case scenario. We live in a society where disgruntled employees do some nasty things. This is why some employers decline two-week notices and tell employees who tender their resignations to leave immediately. If you allow the employee to work out his notice, monitor him closely. One manager gives employees a thank you gift for their service as soon as they tender their resignations. Her reasoning is that this creates a modicum of guilt and decreases the likelihood of vindictiveness.

Regardless of the time frame, get resignations in writing. If not, mail a letter confirming the resignation to the employee's house. Mail two copies to yourself and do not open them. The U.S. Postal Service postmark on the unopened envelopes will serve as sufficient proof that the letter was sent on that date. Should the employee later claim he was fired and file for unemployment benefits, meet with someone in the agency that administers unemployment benefits in your state. Give her one of the unopened envelopes with the postmark on it, and ask her to open it. The dramatic effect is quite compelling in proving the employee was not terminated.

## Laziness

It is human nature to be lazy. Some people insist that work should be fun. Occasionally I meet managers whose companies offer jobs so coveted that they turn applicants away in droves. Gina in Charleston, South Carolina, told me she has people standing in line to work for her. She manages Jimmy Buffett's Margaritaville Store. The manager of the Boothill Saloon in Daytona Beach, Florida, told me they have the same situation. I'm still willing to take Keith Richards' place in the Rolling Stones any time he wants to step aside, and I'll do it for free. Few jobs are that fun, and even fewer are easy. Work is tough. That's why employers have to pay people to do the job. Employees of Kirby Lane restaurant in Austin, Texas, wear shirts that read, "Work tough or go home." Millions of Americans today have never had to work hard. They wouldn't recognize a 60-hour workweek if it bit them. An 80-hour workweek would cause them to have a coronary. Managers know how much work is required to get the job done. The Fair Labor Standards Act created the mentality that 40 hours a week is all that should be expected by requiring employers to pay time and a half to hourly employees who work more than 40 hours in a week. Fortunately, the government doesn't force employers to pay extra money when employees work extra hard. If the problem is laziness, the solution is to not allow it. You buy eight hours of your employee's time each day. Make sure you get what you paid for. You can't make people take initiative, but you can prevent them from goofing off.

## Loaning Money to Employees

Over-indulgent parents who never say no to their children become enablers. The children's material wants grow until they become "gimme, gimme, gimme" machines. It seems unfair in the scheme of things. Mom and dad worked hard to earn the money, and it should be a blessing to the children that the parents can afford to buy them nice things. Instead, it becomes a curse because their kids don't learn limits. They become dependent and expect more in the future. Tom Stanley and William Danko addressed this issue in *The Millionaire Next Door*.[9] They found that parents who loan or give their adult children money greatly decrease the chance of them ever reaching financial independence. Employers make the same mistake by loaning employees money. It sends three messages:

1. I'm not paying you enough.
2. I acknowledge that you're irresponsible.
3. I'm going to enable your financial irresponsibility.

Do bad things happen to good people? Yes. Do people need a helping hand every now and then? Yes. Does this mean the employer should loan an employee money? No! This is not being helpful. You're his employer, not his banker. Loaning money to an employee crosses the boundary into his personal finances. You both need to recognize this boundary and respect it.

## Looking for Another Job on Company Time

I'll never forget Christmas 1989. My company was closed for the week. I was scrolling through computer files and found a resume one of my employees created on my time and on my computer. At first, I was angry. Then I felt betrayed. Then I felt insulted. I saw the movie *Tango & Cash* with Sylvester Stallone and Kurt Russell that night. Every time that movie is rerun on television, I recall that day and all the emotions associated with it. As frustrating as it was, I had no right to feel any of those emotions. I had no policy on personal use of computers. In fact, I did the same thing when I left my last employer.

We can never appreciate what we have until we know what our options are. Interviewing for another job is not always a bad thing. Some companies pay employees $100 for each job offer they bring in. It gives the employer a chance to meet any competing offers and remain competitive in the market. It also exposes employees to what's out there. It's unrealistic not to expect people to better themselves. It is realistic to prohibit them from using your resources to do so. A policy should be created to address the issue.

## Lying

Managers sometimes ask me about managing pathological liars. This term is often used incorrectly to label anyone who repeatedly lies. There's no clinical diagnosis for pathological liars listed in the *Diagnostic and Statistical Manual of Mental Disorders*. Chronic lying in adults is often a manifestation of sociopathic behavior. Sociopaths lack conscience and feel no guilt. Their modus operandi is immediate gratification. Pathological liars will lie to you repeatedly, in spite of its unreasonableness, in response to an obsession.

Don't oversimplify the issue of lying. It's more complicated than most people realize. The biggest lie people tell is that they don't lie. We all lie. One researcher estimates the average American lies three times per day. A retired FBI polygraph examiner explained that lies are social grease sometimes necessary to reduce friction. Not all lies are for the benefit of the liar; some are for the benefit of the person being lied to. Telling lies has a value, and sometimes it's greater than the value of telling the truth. Lying can be the morally right thing to do. If the Nazis came to your house in the 1940s and asked if you were hiding Jews, you would have lied. In Exodus 1:20, God blessed Egyptian midwives after they saved the lives of Hebrew boys by lying to their boss, the King of Egypt. Not only was it a lie, but it was a whopper. They were supposed to kill the boys as soon as they were born. When the king asked why they didn't, they told him they didn't have time because the Hebrew women were much faster at child-birth than Egyptian women. Now there's an example of employees who knew how to think on their feet. These women would have made great lawyers. God directly told Samuel to lie in First Samuel 16:2. Samuel was sent to Bethlehem to find a new king. He knew Saul would be miffed about losing his gig as king. Imagine that you're the general manager and your human resources director comes to visit. You ask why she's there, and she tells you she's inter-viewing applicants to replace you. You wouldn't be a happy camper. Samuel knew Saul would kill him if he knew what brought him to town. When he asked God how he should answer if asked, God told him to lie.

Most situations won't be as drastic as life and death. We all lie for less noble reasons. Parents lie to their own children about Santa Claus and the Easter Bunny. Parents also expect you to lie to them when they show you pictures of their kids. Mothers of young chil-dren are the worst. They'll show you photo after photo after photo. Your first lie is implied by pretending to be interested, when you really want to scream "Enough already!" Then you'll overtly lie by telling her how adorable her kids are, even though you're silently thinking yours are much cuter than hers.

Am I saying it's okay to lie? Absolutely not. It's also not okay to be naïve or hypocritical. Don't expect people to be 100 percent honest with you, 100 percent of the time. People who claim they want total honesty all the time are lying to you and to themselves, even if they don't realize it. No one wants to live in a world where people are so brutally honest that they're hurtful. This is what happened with Jim Carrey in the movie *Liar, Liar*. We want people to be tactfully honest, not brutally honest. While honesty is the best policy, there will be shades of gray. Witnesses in trials swear to tell the whole truth and nothing but the truth. Does anyone really believe they tell the whole truth? Did Bill Clinton tell the whole truth when he said he didn't have "sexual relations" with Monica Lewinsky?

This discussion is not about right or wrong; it's about reality. There are consequences to telling the truth to authority figures. This is why your kids will share things with each other that they'd never share with you. You are an authority figure in your child's life. You're also an authority figure in your employee's life. I take a hard-line on holding people accountable. I also take a hard-line on managers staying in touch with reality. Don't get too caught up in self-righteous indignation and act surprised when you discover an employee has been less than 100 percent honest with you. Hold everyone accountable, but be realistic in your expectations. People are going to lie to you whether or not you are prepared for it, so prepare for it.

## Managing Off-Site Employees

It's difficult to monitor employees when no one is present to do the monitoring. The geographic distance is not the issue; it's the loss of personal interaction. Supervision is a hands-on process. The less interaction we have with an employee, the less effectively we can supervise. Distance makes it easier for us to be fooled. We see this on the Internet when people lie about themselves in chat rooms. While people can and do lie in person, at least personal interaction allows confirmation that a 19-year-old girl is not a 55-year-old man.

I met a cab driver in New Orleans, Louisiana, who took the importance of personal interaction more seriously than anyone I've ever met. He proudly told me how he brought his family to the United States from the Dominican Republic in the 1980s, and that each of his three children went to college. His two oldest attended local colleges, while his youngest daughter earned a scholarship to a university 900 miles away. He and his wife are proud, but concerned about their daughter living so far from home. Even though they talk to her by phone every day, they drive 14 hours to see her once a month. I asked why they go to such extremes. He explained that talking to her is not enough. He and his wife want to look her in the eyes. By seeing her in person, they could tell if she had been drinking, eating right, and getting enough rest. They know teenagers can easily get into trouble when they're so far from home, and the thought of Mom and Dad coming to visit every month can be a deterrent to temptations that might arise. Every time I hear about college students drinking themselves to death, I think about the cab driver. He deserves a Dr. Laura shirt with "I am my kid's Dad" more than any man I've ever met. He understands that parenting from a distance requires extra effort.

Managing from a distance also requires extra effort. A trend called telecommuting became popular in the 1990s. Companies began allowing certain administrative employees to work from home a few days per week, using e-mail, the Internet, and phones to stay connected to the office. For most organizations, this is asking for unnecessary trouble. People will rarely be as productive at home as they are at the office. The first danger is the increased possibility of cyber loafing or excessive personal phone conversations. Even when an employee is focused on his task and these are not issues, a home environment creates distractions that don't exist in the office. I am a prime example. I'm more prolific when I'm writing in my office than when I'm writing at home. My brain is conditioned to go into work mode when I walk into the office and see my name on the door. When I'm at home, I see a light bulb that needs changing, car that needs washing, or hear Attila the Hun, my next-door neighbor's rottweiler, raising a ruckus. My first advice on managing employees who work from home is not to allow telecommuting. If you are going to allow it, do so only with employees who have earned your trust and proven they are highly disciplined and focused. The key is to focus on results. As long as the work is done in an acceptable manner, everything's fine. Each one of JetBlue Airways' 700 reservationists works from home in the Salt Lake City, Utah area. This works for them, but they are an exception to the rule.

In some industries, managing from a distance is unavoidable. Sales representatives, plumbers, air conditioning and refrigeration technicians, carpet installers, home health care workers, and delivery drivers often work unsupervised. The ideal solution is using a GPS to monitor routes and times. If this is not possible, constant phone interaction is an absolute necessity. As with telecommuters, managing employees who make service or sales calls requires extra effort. Never underestimate the importance of personal interaction with the employees you supervise.

## Motivating Slackers

Managers ask me "What motivates people?" My response is "Motivate whom to do what?" The question is analogous to asking, "What is the meaning of life?" It's too broad and too vague to answer specifically. There are two broad categories that motivate everyone. Every choice we make and every action we take is out of the desire for pleasure, or the avoidance of pain. Specific motivators are different for each person. You must determine this on a case-by-case basis.

While we don't know any one specific motivator that works on everyone, we know one that doesn't work as a primary, long-term motivator: money. Money is too intangible. A check for $1,000,000 is the same size as a check for $2. This is why receiving money as a birthday or Christmas gift is never as fulfilling as most people think. It's not the gift that counts; it's the thought. Writing a check doesn't require much thought or effort. Imagine you budgeted $50 to buy a Christmas present for someone you love. Buying her anything requires more effort than writing a check for $50. Some will argue, "But Glenn, if I'm expecting a pair of socks from my grandmother and she gives me a check for $1,000, I'm going to be very happy." You would be happy because the gift exceeded your expectations. Had you expected a $1,000 check and received a $1,000 check, you would have already taken the money for granted before you received it. It would be one of those awkward Christmas moments when you pretend to be surprised and grateful on the outside, while thinking "Ho Hum" on the inside.

Money is only a temporary motivator. No matter how much of a raise you give your employees, it will eventually lose its value. They'll take it for granted and want more. Money does two things long term. First, it attracts new employees. If you run an ad in the Sunday paper offering $14 an hour for a position that could be filled by individuals currently making $8 an hour, you'll be overwhelmed with applicants Monday morning. Second, money reduces turnover.

People who would normally work for $8 an hour will stick with a $14 an hour job because they don't want to take a 43 percent pay cut. Money attracts employees on the front end and keeps them on the back end, but does little to motivate them in-between.

Sometimes money can be a better motivator when an employee is already extremely well paid. Let's revisit the small town police department from Chapter 5, where new officers start at $52,000 a year. The assistant chief asked how to motivate a rookie police officer who makes more than he would at most other jobs. This is similar to the age-old dilemma of what to buy someone for Christmas when he already has everything. The answer is that you can't buy anything meaningful for someone who already has everything. The same is true for employees. You can't give meaningful rewards to an employee who is already so generously rewarded. You can, however, motivate the employee. The motivator for a highly paid employee is the fear of losing his high-paying job. The assistant chief told me 28 police officers from other towns applied for the last four open positions in his department. If an employee takes a high paying job for granted, he won't be motivated to work hard to keep the job. If he thinks his high paying job may be in jeopardy, he'll be motivated to keep it.

Everyone is motivated by something. Managers must take the time and make the effort to figure out what that something is for each employee.

## Perfectionism

Perfectionism can be a form of obsessive-compulsive behavior. It's more of a problem with managers than subordinates. Managers sometimes insist their field requires high standards. One can demand high standards without being a perfectionist. Sister Barbara Jean attended my seminar in Cleveland, Ohio. She works at a retirement home for nuns, and told me that cleanliness really is next to godliness in her case. One drop of water on the terrazine floor could mean a broken leg for some of the frail residents who can hardly walk across the floor. This is not perfectionism; this is a high standard which is a necessity. Most jobs don't require standards this high. Perfectionist managers demand *unreasonably* high standards.

They obsess over irrelevant details, nitpick, and hyperfocus on sometimes-irrelevant mistakes, making themselves and their employees miserable in the process. There's nothing wrong with being the best we can be. Striving for the impossible, however, is mentally unhealthy. Perfectionist managers have a strong tendency to over control and see things as black or white. They don't see the shades of gray in-between. Consequently, they lose touch with reality. Perfectionism is the opposite of carelessness. While careless people miss details, perfectionists place too much emphasis on details.

The cure for perfectionism is to lower your standards. Don't throw them out the window altogether; simply lower them to something reasonable. It's more important to be reasonable than to be right. If you think it's unacceptable to lower your standards in business, I have two words to prove you wrong: Microsoft Windows. Can you name one computer user who hasn't experienced a crash caused by Windows? Microsoft regularly announces glitches in their product after they've sold it to millions of customers. Yet, Bill Gates remains the wealthiest person in the world. He's not the wealthiest because he's the smartest, the most educated, or because his company has higher quality standards than others. It's because he hustled and got things done. He didn't do them perfectly, but he got them done. This is what managers have to do. Because management is about getting things done, managers have to set standards that are reasonably attainable. Perfectionist managers have to learn that a good enough job that is completed is better than a perfect job that drags on forever.

## Political Correctness

Larry Burkett said that if a married couple agrees 100 percent of the time, one of them is unnecessary. You and your spouse don't agree 100 percent of the time, but you don't divorce because of it. Yet, political correctness has lead people to believe that if someone doesn't agree with them 100 percent of the time, they can call him or her names like sexist, racist, mean-spirited, redneck, Neanderthal, or bigot. Political correctness was supposed to make people more tolerant, but it has caused some to become less tolerant. For example, just because someone says "Black" instead of "African American" does not mean he's a racist. It just means he uses a different term. A woman who immigrated to the United States from South Africa told me she uses Black for a different reason. She said, "I lived in Africa for 20 years. I have lived in America for 10 years. I am African American." She was as White as me and had an excellent point. She's not a racist; she just has a different perspective.

I can work with people regardless of whether they're Black or White, straight or gay, religious or atheist, male or female, conservative or liberal. I cannot work with narrow-minded people who believe everyone has to think exactly like them. We don't have to agree 100 percent of the time. We do have to work with others who don't agree with us. When employees see everything with tunnel vision, tell them, "You don't have to agree with my beliefs and I don't have to agree with yours. We do have to respect each other's rights to have beliefs. If you can't accept this, you may be happier working elsewhere."

## "Poor Pitiful Me" Syndrome

Healthy employees seek recognition for what they accomplish. "Poor Pitiful Me" (PPM) employees seek recognition for what has happened to them. They crave sympathy so much that they'll compete for it. A PPM person will one-up anyone who dares mention his or her own suffering. You'll hear comments like "If you think you had it bad, let me tell you what happened to me." Achievement empowers people and causes them to grow. Self-pity debilitates people and causes them to wither. PPM becomes an excuse to avoid accountability. You've heard people say, "Can you just cut me a little slack?" PPM people cut slack for themselves.

They can't form healthy relationships because they can't give; they only know how to take. They aren't good team players because they can't contribute to a team. This book is about taking responsibility and holding people accountable. However, there are times when people stumble. Bad things happen to good people. Employees get cancer, their spouses have open-heart surgery, and their parents die. We all have a moral responsibility to help those in need during difficult times. PPM people can't fulfill this responsibility because they're too consumed with feeling sorry for themselves.

They also destroy any healthy relationships they might already have. It becomes a vicious cycle. The more they feel sorry for themselves, the more they destroy relationships. The more they destroy relationships, the more they feel sorry for themselves. The best solution for dealing with PPM people is to hold them accountable, and managers are in the perfect position to do this. First, don't let them wallow in self-pity. The next time an employee says something like "That's just my luck," respond with, "I would feel sorry for you, but you're doing such a good job of feeling sorry for yourself, I don't think I can keep up." Second, don't cut slack where it isn't due. When constantly wallowing in self-pity no longer achieves the desired results, it loses its appeal for the PPM person.

## Resistance to Change

Some people are allergic to change. They automatically oppose anything new or different. There are two common solutions to this problem. The first is called the horror floor. Imagine that you won a trip to New York City, and you're excited about it. Your stubborn employee says, "You don't want to go to New York City. The crime rate is awful and you'll get mugged, or worse." Years ago, New York was a dangerous place to visit. Today, it's safer than many small towns across America. Your employee has an old image ingrained in his head. No matter how much you argue the point, you won't win. Instead, pull out the horror floor by attacking the worst-case scenario and working backward. Ask him "What's the worst that could happen?" Once he says you could be murdered, he can no longer one-up you. He's already used his most powerful argument. Respond with "People are murdered in small towns every day. If this weekend is my time to go, I'd like to go out in style in New York City!" You just beat him at his own game.

The second method is called desensitization. People who reject change feel threatened by it. An example managers often experience is computers. Announce you're bringing computers in for the first time, and you're likely to encounter some resistance. People who aren't comfortable with computers might feel like their value to the company will be diminished. Don't try to teach employees who lack computer literacy how to use spreadsheets or word processors the first day. Start slowly by having them turn the computer on, learn to use a mouse, or play a game. Slowly desensitize them before you throw them into a complex program that may be intimidating and reinforce their resistance to the change. As they become more comfortable with the basics, add a word processing program. Then work forward as they become more comfortable and confident. Use baby steps as discussed in Chapter 2.

## Slow Pokes

Several factors can cause an employee to be slower than others. Reasons can include lack of manual dexterity, age, perfectionism, or lack of focus. Working slower than others can be a hindrance in an office. It can be a financial disaster in manufacturing with the bottlenecking problem discussed in Chapter 8. When 300 employees are on a production line, each must work at the same pace to keep from backing up others. The employee in the most downstream position will hold up the other 299 if he can't keep up with the others. One solution is peer pressure. Another is retraining. There is also the fundamental question of whether the employee is capable of doing the job in the first place. When someone isn't working fast enough, the question is whether he's unable or unwilling. Either way, he has to keep up with the team. If he doesn't, his lack of productivity is multiplied times the number of people he is slowing down. The problem must be dealt with swiftly.

## Substance Abuse

As we discussed in Chapter 4, substance abusers cost their employers about twice as much in medical and worker's comp claims as nonusers. They are 2½ times more likely to be absent eight or more days a year. Drug testing applicants is a smart idea. Drug testing existing employees is even smarter. The Substance Abuse and Mental Health Services Administration reports 70 percent of illicit drug users age 18 to 49 are employed full time.

Alcohol is a different matter. It is not illegal, but it can still have a devastating impact on employers. The U.S. Department of Labor web site (www.dol.gov) states that 1 in 5 workers report having to work harder, redo work, cover for a coworker, or have been put in danger or injured as a result of a fellow employee's drinking.[10] It also states that up to 40 percent of industrial fatalities and 47 percent of industrial injuries can be linked to alcohol consumption or alcoholism.[11] Imagine that an employee comes to work staggering. You can smell alcohol on his breath. You think he's been drinking, but he denies it. Legally, you have nothing until you get proof. Require all employees to agree to testing any time they're asked. As a condition of employment, all employees should sign a consent form at the time of hiring. They should agree to alcohol level testing anytime they are involved in an accident, behave suspiciously, or are randomly selected. The consent form should also state that refusing to submit would be construed as a resignation. Many employers today use field tests as an initial indication of whether an employee needs to be taken to a lab for further testing. Disposable alcohol detectors such as BreathScan are about the size of a cigarette and cost around $3. They are available from most companies that sell HR supplies, such as www.gneil.com. These are not a substitute for a licensed testing laboratory or hospital, but can provide an excellent first line of defense. Have your attorney help create the policy and testing procedure.

## Task Avoidance

Task avoidance refers to the employee who cherry-picks the pleasant tasks. He does a good job at tasks he enjoys, but completely avoids the ones he dislikes. Pretend you're a heating and air conditioning contractor. You employ an HVAC technician whose technical skills are outstanding. He loves repairing and installing heating and air conditioning systems, but hates returning to the warehouse each day to replenish supplies on his truck. He constantly has to leave jobsites and drive back to the warehouse or nearest Lowe's store to purchase supplies. His avoidance of unpleasant tasks will eventually overshadow his outstanding technical skills. Doing the job well means doing the entire job, not just the pleasant parts. You don't want to hear a pilot announce, "Ladies and gentlemen, I enjoy departures but don't like the hassle of landing the plane. I'll do it eventually, but I'm taking a coffee break right now." You expect him to perform the entire job from beginning to end, and on schedule. You should expect your employees to do the same. An employee who performs only the tasks he enjoys is not a good employee. He's going through the large bag of potato chips and eating the big ones, leaving the small chips and crumbs for everyone else. Allowing an employee to cherry-pick pleasant tasks punishes good employees who have to complete the unpleasant tasks for him. Write him up for task avoidance and explain that his job is in jeopardy if he does not fulfill all his duties, including the ones he dislikes.

## Tattletales

Dictionary.com defines tattle as "to reveal the plans or activities of another, gossip, to chatter aimlessly." When employees tattle on others, it could be more than gossip. Gossip is more about rumors and is of a more intimate nature. It can even be a lie. If the tattletale is reporting legitimate information, managers should discern whether the end justifies the means. It's not tattling when Roxanne tells you Margaret is embezzling. This is reporting behavior she has a professional, moral, and legal obligation to report. When Roxanne walks all the way down the hall to tell you Margaret clocked in two minutes late, it is tattling. Chances are that Roxanne wasted more than two minutes of her time coming to your office to tell you about Margaret. It may be true that Margaret clocked in two minutes late. You'll deal with this issue in your own time. At this exact moment, Roxanne has wasted as much time as Margaret. Since Roxanne is the one standing in front of your desk, she's the one you should deal with first.

## That's Not in My Job Description

Imagine you walked into the breakroom where John just finished a Coca-Cola. He crushes the can and tosses it across the room into the wastebasket. The wastebasket is already overflowing, the can tumbles onto the floor, and he walks away. You suggest that he pick the can up and put it in the wastebasket where it belongs. He informs you it will do no good because the wastebasket is full, and the can will fall off again. You suggest he empty the wastebasket, and he responds, "That's not in my job description." Resist the temptation to say, "It is now." When he says it's not in his job description, he's implying he doesn't have to do anything that's not written in a job description. You can't possibly write down every single task your employees are expected to do. Instead, respond, "I expect all employees to perform certain tasks when the need arises, without being told to do them. It's called taking initiative, and I expect you to take initiative." You just held John to a higher level of professionalism than he's holding himself.

## The Meddling Spouse

Medical practice managers often tell me about the doctor's wife who gets involved just enough to interfere, but not enough to help. The problem occurs because she's only there sporadically. She's there long enough to create problems, but is nowhere to be found when it's time to solve them. She wants to be a full-time mom, and tries to be a part-time manager. Because she sticks to no set schedule, employees don't know whom to turn to when they have questions. Managers can't be part-time any more than parents can be part-time. It's fine for husbands or wives to work part-time in their spouse's business as long as their role is clearly defined. This role can be just about anything other than manager. The wife of a urologist in New Hampshire took great offense to this. She enjoyed coming and going whenever she chose. Her argument was that since the last name on the building was the same as hers, she was part owner of the practice. She may have been part owner, but she still can't be a part manager. Paris Hilton's last name is on over 2,000 hotels, but employees don't want her to walk in and start ordering them around. Owning a business and running a business are two separate things. It's okay for the owner's spouse to manage. It's also okay for the spouse to work part-time. It's not okay to do both. The spouse has to choose one or the other.

## The Peter Principle

Sometimes an employee has a good attitude and tries his best, but just can't do the job. There are three solutions:

1. Retrain him.
2. Assign him a mentor.
3. Move him to a different position.

Dr. Laurence J. Peter was the first to point out that people are promoted to their level of incompetence. Today this is called "The Peter Principle." Imagine William is the best sales rep the company has ever employed. He sold more copy machines than any salesman in company history. He's promoted to sales manager and is fantastic. Next, he's promoted to general manager. Now in addition to sales, he's also responsible for accounting, marketing, research, and personnel. He was never responsible for this many tasks before, and is a miserable failure. He can't handle personnel problems and doesn't understand accounting or finance. Because he was so productive as a sales rep and sales manager, the company doesn't want to terminate him. If they can't move him back down the ladder, he'll stay pigeonholed in the position of general manager for the rest of his tenure with the company. Letting someone go because you promoted him or her too far is difficult. If there's no other place to move him or her, it may be the only choice.

## Toxic Personalities

People with toxic personalities can be pleasant when they're forced to be. A toxic person may behave around his mother-in-law because she intimidates him. He then misbehaves around his wife and kids because he knows he can get away with it. An employee who has a toxic personality may not change his personality, but will behave at work if he knows you won't tolerate his bad behavior. You can give him permission to be toxic, or you can set boundaries and enforce them.

Not allowing toxic people to infect your organization pays off in numerous ways. The manager of a dental office in North Carolina discovered this when she finally put her foot down with a troubled hygienist. The hygienist had been allowed to spew venom for years. As a result, several good employees left to go work in organizations with more pleasant working conditions. One departing employee even told her, "Life is too short to be so miserable." When she finally fired the toxic employee, her other employees were elated. Then came the task of hiring the replacement. The manager interviewed a hygienist who knew the receptionist. She said, "I heard how you didn't put up with any crap here and I like that." She ultimately did not hire that individual, but her reputation immediately helped in her recruiting effort. Don't allow toxic people to suck the energy out of their coworkers.

## Ungratefulness

Managers ask me why people don't appreciate having a job. There are four reasons. The first is because of the entitlement mentality. People think the world owes them something. When people think they're owed something, they won't be grateful for receiving it. Second, people take good jobs for granted because they're so abundant. Third, people lack the basic social graces discussed in Chapter 3. Being grateful is a form of good manners, which many people today never learned. Fourth, some people aren't smart enough to realize the personal benefits of being grateful to others. Even if someone really isn't grateful, a gesture of gratitude can be beneficial. Let's go back to the example of the socks you received from your grandmother every Christmas. Everyone knows that socks given to a child are really a gift to the child's mother so she won't have to buy them, but you knew to play along. You gave Grandma a big hug and thanked her because you knew she would spoil you rotten throughout the year. Yet adults often forget the importance of showing gratitude.

I send out over 100 boxes of chocolate covered cherries to colleagues each Christmas, and can count on one hand the number who bother to acknowledge receiving them. I answer thousands of e-mailed questions from seminar attendees each year, and receive an acknowledgment from about 5 out of each 100 I answer. I tried to rationalize this by reasoning the managers were too busy to thank me, but my reasoning fails every time I get backlogged. People always find time to complain if I don't reply immediately. It never occurs to them that I have paying clients and don't have endless hours to give out free advice, or hundreds of others e-mails may be in front of theirs. As soon as I answer their question, I never hear from them again. I have also found that the ones who complain when I don't reply immediately are the least likely to thank me when I do reply.

While it would be nice if people appreciated what we do for them, most won't. This is a battle I have never found a way to win. The best answer I can find personally is to make sure I don't give too much of myself, while at the same time not compromise my professional standards. The best answer I can find for employers is to pay employees fairly and consider the account settled in full. Anything more is a gift.

## Video Monitoring of Employees

Employers monitor workers for two reasons. One is for security, and the other is the Hawthorne Effect. As discussed in Chapter 3, behavior improves when people know, or merely think, they are being monitored. An online poll conducted by SHRM and CareerJournal.com found that 22 percent of employers have used cameras to monitor employee activities.[12] The bottom line on video monitoring is that it works. The legal side is another matter. Even though employers generally have this right, there have been lawsuits. One hotel in West Virginia was sued for six figures after video monitoring employees at the check-in counter, even though the employees were aware they were being monitored. Video monitoring can improve performance and decrease theft, but it must be set up within the boundaries of the law. Check with your attorney before installing video cameras.

## Workaholism

Working with great intensity for a period of time in order to achieve a specific goal is focus. This is healthy and productive. Constantly working obsessively for no good reason is workaholism.

This is unhealthy and can actually be counter productive. In the long run, workaholics accomplish less because they work less efficiently. They start to resent their jobs, and spend as much time complaining as working. One golf pro in Louisiana told me the first question he asks job applicants is, "Do you have a life?" If they answer yes, he tells them not to work for him. I made the mistake of being a workaholic until I read *The Millionaire Next Door*, and learned the average self-made millionaire is not a workaholic. They pay their dues by putting in plenty of long days when necessary, but keep things in balance. As Paul Harvey says, "All things in moderation." Look closely at employees who work through lunch and stay late every day. Their productivity is usually not commensurate with their hours. The key is to focus on results instead of activity. This also applies to managers. Managers are notorious for coming in on weekends to "catch up" because of their heavy workloads. In reality, the reason they need to work weekends is not because of all the work they did Monday through Friday, but because of the work they didn't do, but could have done Monday through Friday. They are simply inefficient and have no incentive to be more efficient as long as they're willing to work constantly. If you have employees who fall under this category, start by making them take a lunch break. Also make everyone use vacation time each year. There's a time to work, and a time to rest. This applies to both management and nonmanagement employees.

## Working on Holidays

There are legal issues regarding employers who force employees to work on religious holy days. Friday is a holy day in the Islamic religion and employers must make some sort of accommodation. An Illinois company that refused an Islamic employee's request paid $49,000 to settle a discrimination claim. Most traditional American holidays, however, are not considered holy days. Numerous managers have told me about employees who raise a ruckus about working on Christmas Day, even though their religion doesn't even recognize Christmas. Parents with small children will want off on Christmas Eve and Christmas Day, but it's usually more of a family issue than a religious one. I voluntarily worked on this book on Thanksgiving Day, Christmas Day, and New Year's Day, and my life didn't suffer. I would have preferred to play golf, shoot skeet, or go flying, but I had a deadline to meet. I'll have plenty of time to play when the book is finished.

Sometimes working on holidays is only a rivalry between employees. Employees don't want to work on a day others have off. The truth is that many Americans will spend Christmas and Thanksgiving Day sitting around the house, entertaining relatives they don't like, and getting so bored that they sleep through much of it. I suspect there are more than a few people who might actually be happier working holidays. Firefighters, police officers, doctors, nurses, and professional football players have no choice but to work on holidays. Even if your employees do have a choice, getting them to volunteer sometimes requires less effort than employers might think. The manager of a Nashville restaurant informed me they paid triple time to employees who would work Christmas Day until 1994. They then dropped it to double time, and eventually to time and a half. Some people volunteer to work without pay on these days. David Letterman spent Christmas Day 2004 entertaining American troops in Afghanistan and handing out 5,000 shirts that read "Late Show Afghanistan." People work holidays regardless of whether they are celebrities or servers. Some companies offer employees the choice of working Christmas or Thanksgiving, while others rotate from year to year. If your organization is open on holidays, make it clear that someone has to work. The world does not stop turning because they do.

## Your Own Family Members

Employing your own children is a tradition that helped build our country. When we were still primarily an agricultural society in the first century of our existence, the family farm grew as more children were born. Today, business owners in every industry employ their own children. However, the lack of discipline in many homes today means it's not always a good idea. If your children respect your authority at home, supervising them at work should be natural. If they don't respect your authority at home, leave them there.

Supervising your own parents brings the priceless asset of unshakable loyalty. This works as long as there's no power play. If your parents founded the company, the line of succession must be clear. It's critical for employees to know who's in charge. If power struggles erupt, the organization will function more like a clogged toilet than a well-oiled machine.

Your ability to supervise your own siblings depends on how clearly the hierarchy of authority is defined. If petty sibling rivalries and jealousy emerge, it will be impossible. At work, you are no longer a baby brother or big sister. You are the manager, regardless of your birth order.

Supervising your own spouse is wrought with peril. A 53-year-old insurance agent who worked with his wife told me he was so miserable that he wanted to run away from home. He didn't have a management problem; he had a marital problem. The biggest problem for spouses who work together usually isn't the relationship; it's defining where work life stops and home life begins. If you work with your spouse, agree on a boundary to protect your marriage. Some couples set a specific time. For example, after 9:00 P.M., no shoptalk is allowed. Anyone who breaks the rule has to do dishes, give a back rub, or pay whatever penance the other chooses.

Business owners ask if it's necessary to create a paper trail on their own spouse or children. It's even more important than with other employees, but for a different reason. The reason to create a paper trail on other employees is to clearly communicate to the employee when his or her job is in jeopardy. The manager should then keep the paperwork to prove the employee knew his job was in jeopardy. The reason a business owner should keep a paper trail on his own wife or children is to communicate to himself when they need to go. It's impossible to remain objective with family members. Some managers are biased in favor of their family members; this is nepotism. Others are unfairly harsh. One small business owner asked, "How could I justify firing the mother of my three beautiful children?" My answer was, "Easily, when it's in her best interest and yours." She has a vested interest in the success of the company. If she's being unproductive or disruptive, she'll benefit by finding somewhere else to work.

## Conclusion

There is no one best solution to any of the challenges problem employees pose. Even if there was, what works today might not work 10 years from now. Because society's attitudes and values change with every new generation, it is important for managers to keep up with the changing workforce. Poor managers continue using outdated tactics that worked years ago, and wonder why they no longer work. Good managers adjust their management styles to keep up with the changes. Great managers take proactive steps to stay ahead of imminent changes in the workforce, and anticipate new ones. For this reason, you are to be commended. You have taken at least two proactive steps toward being the best manager you can be. First, you bought this book to enhance your knowledge. It doesn't matter whether you read Peter Drucker, Stephen Covey, myself, or anyone else. What matters is that you made the effort to improve and keep your skills up to date. This is more than most managers do. Charlie "Tremendous" Jones says that we will be the same people five years from now, except for the books we read and the people we meet. You have obviously made the commitment to be a better manager tomorrow than you were yesterday. Second, you are to be commended for completing this book. Many people buy books with the intention of reading them, but never do. You did more than have good intentions; you followed through. This places you even further ahead of so many other managers.

Should you have questions or comments, you can e-mail them to me by going to my web site at www.glennshepard.com. I hope to meet you in person at a live seminar one day. Until then, thank you for keeping our country strong and making it the greatest place on earth to work and live.

# Notes

## Chapter 1: What Happened to the American Work Ethic?

1. Federal Housing Finance Board, monthly press release on November 30, 2004 (FHFB 04-43 MIRS).
2. *Bates v. State Bar of Arizona,* 433 U.S. 350.
3. U.S. Census 2000 Special Reports: Married-Couple and Unmarried-Partner Households.
4. Demos, "Borrowing to Make Ends Meet," Briefing Paper #2, October 2004.
5. As stated in an interview on CBS Evening News, 1/08/04.
6. Data are from the Integrated Public Use Microdata Series Extracts (IPUMS) of the 1960 and 2000 U.S. Censuses. Steven Ruggles, Matthew Sobek, Trent Alexander, Catherine A. Fitch, Ronald Goeken, Patricia Kelly Hall, Miriam King, and Chad Ronnander. *Integrated Public Use Microdata Series: Version 3.0* [Machine-readable database]. Minneapolis, MN: Minnesota Population Center [producer and distributor], 2004.
7. Nellie Mae 2002 National Student Loan Survey, Final Report February 6, 2003.
8. Synovate, "Where's Mom and Dad?" September 2004.
9. Larry Winget (Hoboken, NJ: John Wiley & Sons, 2004).
10. John T. Malloy (New York: Warner Books, 1988).
11. Peter F. Drucker with Joseph A. Maciariello (New York: Harper Business, 2004).
12. *Petermann v. International Brotherhood of Teamsters,* supra, 174 Cal.App.2d.
13. *Cleary v. American Airlines, Inc.* (1980) 111 Cal.App.3d 443.

## Chapter 2: Becoming the Manager You Need to Be

1. The Business Source, 2003, Franklin, TN.
2. "Parenting With Pills," first broadcast on the Dr. Phil show September 28, 2004.

## Chapter 4: How Do I Avoid Hiring Problem Employees?

1. U.S. Department of Health and Human Services National Institute on Drug Abuse, September 24, 2002, NIDA InfoFacts: Workplace Trends Washington, DC: U.S. Government Printing Office.
2. As published on the U.S. Department of Labor's website at www.dol.gov/asp.

## Chapter 6: How to Avoid Legal Pitfalls

1. *Gilmer v. Interstate/Johnson Lane Corp.*, 500 U.S. 20, 111 S.Ct. 1647.
2. *Hooters of America Inc. v. Phillips*, Case 173 F3d 933.
3. *EEOC v. Waffle House, Inc.*, (99-1823) 534 U.S. 279, 193 F.3d 805.
4. *EEOC v. Allstate Insurance Company*, E.D. Pa. 2004.
5. "Background Checks and Resume Inaccuracies," *SHRM Weekly Survey*, April 27, 2004.
6. Walnut Creek, CA: The Management Advantage, 1999.

## Chapter 8: How to Get Employees to Come to Work and Be on Time

1. Hoboken, NJ: John Wiley & Sons, to be published in 2006.

## Chapter 9: The Art of Discipline

1. Spencer Johnson (New York: Penguin Putnam, 1998).

## Chapter 11: How to Handle Daily Challenges Problem Employees Create

1. "Policies About Cell Phone Use in the Workplace," *SHRM Weekly Survey*, April 20, 2004.
2. Hoboken, NJ: John Wiley & Sons, 2003.
3. "2003 E-mail Rules, Policies, and Practices Survey" conducted by the American Management Association, The ePolicy Institute, and Clearswift.
4. New York: Simon & Schuster, 1990.
5. You can contact AT&T interpretation services at www.languageline.com or 800-752-6096.
6. "Workplace Privacy," October 2004.
7. New York: McGraw Hill, 2003.
8. New York: Warner Books, 1996.
9. New York: Pocket Books, a division of Simon & Schuster, 1996.
10. T. W. Mangione, J. Howland, and M. Lee. "Alcohol and Work: Results from a Corporate Drinking Study," in *To Improve Health and Health Care: 1998–1999*, ed. S. L. Isaacs and J. R. Knickerman (San Francisco: Jossey-Bass, 1998).
11. M. Bernstein, and J. Mahoney, "Management Perspectives on Alcoholism: The Employer's Stake in Alcoholism Treatment." *Occupational Medicine*, 4(2), 1989.
12. October 2004.

# Index